Turkey: America's Forgotten Ally

Turkey

America's Forgotten Ally

Dankwart A. Rustow

COUNCIL ON FOREIGN RELATIONS PRESS

NEW YORK • LONDON

COUNCIL ON FOREIGN RELATIONS BOOKS

The Council on Foreign Relations, Inc., is a nonprofit and nonpartisan organization devoted to promoting improved understanding of international affairs through the free exchange of ideas. The Council does not take any position on questions of foreign policy and has no affiliation with, and receives no funding from, the United States government.

From time to time, books and monographs written by members of the Council's research staff or visiting fellows, or commissioned by the Council, or written by an independent author with critical review contributed by a Council study or working group are published with the designation "Council on Foreign Relations Book." Any book or monograph bearing that designation is, in the judgement of the Committee on Studies of the Council's Board of Directors, a responsible treatment of a significant international topic worthy of presentation to the public. All statements of fact and expressions of opinion contained in Council books are, however, the sole responsibility of the author.

Copyright © 1987, 1989 by the Council on Foreign Relations, Inc.
All rights reserved.
Printed in the United States of America.

This book may not be reproduced, in whole or in part, in any form (beyond that copying permitted by Sections 107 and 108 of the U.S. Copyright Law and excerpts by reviewers for the public press), without written permission from the publishers. For information, write Publications Office, Council on Foreign Relations, 58 East 68th Street, New York, NY 10021.

Library of Congress Cataloguing-in-Publication Data

Rustow, Dankwart A.
    Turkey, America's forgotten ally.

    Bibliography: p.
    Includes index.
        1. Turkey—Economic conditions—1960—
2. Turkey—Economic policy. 3. Turkey—Politics and government—1960—
. 4. Turkey—Foreign relations—
United States. 5. United States—Foreign relations—
Turkey. I. Title.
HC 492.R87 1989   330.9561'048   89-7727
ISBN 0-87609-065-X (pbk.)

89 90 91 92 93 94 95 PB 10 9 8 7 6 5 4 3 2 1

Contents

Foreword

Since the end of World War II, the main strategic role of Turkey, as seen by her Western allies and by some elements at least among her southern neighbors, was to serve as a barrier; more specifically, to block the path of Soviet expansion into the Middle East. It is in large measure thanks to the existence and effectiveness of the Turkish barrier that Soviet successes in the Arab countries, though often great, were always precarious, leaving the rulers of those countries the option of reducing or even eliminating Soviet influence if they so chose. This was an option that countries like Poland, Czechoslovakia, Hungary, and more recently Afghanistan—all situated on the frontier or within easy reach of the Soviet Union—do not have. Several Middle Eastern governments which at various times flirted with the Soviet Union, and some of which acted as hosts to Soviet troops and even bases, have been able to terminate that relationship at will, precisely because they were protected from direct Soviet intervention by the land barrier of what was once known as "the Northern Tier." When Sadat decided to expel the Soviet advisers and technicians in 1972, he could do so with impunity, and so too could other rulers in the Middle East if and when they deemed it expedient. Their choice is still determined by expediency, not constraint, and the assessment and determination are their own.

The "Northern Tier" at one time stretched from the eastern Mediterranean to central Asia, and included Greece, Turkey, and Iran, flanked in the east by a neutral Afghanistan. Greece and Turkey were both members of NATO. Turkey, Iran and, from 1955 to 1959, Iraq were part of a Middle East defensive alliance extending to Pakistan. Afghanistan's neutrality was respected on all sides.

The situation today is very different. Afghanistan, after the Communist coup of 1978 and the Soviet invasion of 1979, is no longer neutral but is part of the Soviet orbit. And although Soviet rule is under constant challenge, the Russians have established bases and control the main routes, with new and easy access to the Indian Ocean and to the vulnerable Baluchi borders of both Pakistan and Iran. At the other end of the Tier, Greece, though still a member of NATO and host to American bases, has become, to say the least, a somewhat unpredictable ally.

In Iran, until 1979 the centerpiece of the Middle East defensive system, events have taken a very different course. Iran is certainly not in the Soviet orbit, nor are its present rulers likely to choose such a course. It is, however, an immediate neighbor of the Soviet Union, and the border provinces both on the eastern and on the western sides of the Caspian Sea are inhabited by people of the same language and culture as their Soviet neighbors with whom, indeed, they shared a common fate until the Russian imperial expansion into these areas in the nineteenth century. Massive Soviet forces are poised on the northern borders of Iran, and the defense of Soviet Azerbaijan and Turkmenistan might require, in Soviet strategic thinking, an advance into at least northern Iran—by the same reasoning that the defense of Leningrad requires the control of Warsaw, and the defense of Warsaw control of Prague. The Soviets are familiar with the invasion routes into Iran, and the Russo-Persian treaty of friendship of 1921, still held valid by the Soviet government, provides that in certain circumstances, "Russia shall have the right to advance her troops into the Persian interior for the purpose of carrying out the military operations necessary for its defense" (Article VI). In the event of a breakdown of order in Iran—a not impossible postrevolutionary contingency—even a peacefully inclined Soviet government might consider itself obliged to intervene. In the meantime, while Iran's rulers profess hostility to both superpowers, it is the remote Western threat, rather than the near Soviet threat, to which they find it expedient to give their main attention.

These changes leave Turkey and Greece as the only surviving sections of the northern barrier. Turkey's importance and endangerment are both correspondingly increased. Turkey now has a crucial role to play in the defense of southeastern Europe, the eastern Mediterranean, the Middle East, and even southern Asia. Even Turkey was for some time the target of a very determined effort—organized in large measure from the territory of her northern and southern neighbors—to destabilize the Turkish government and indeed Turkish society, and thus to eliminate Turkey as a political and military factor in the region. There were times when this attempt seemed on the point of success. It was, however, stopped by the intervention of the military, and Turkey is once again ruled by a government which is able to maintain order and stability at home, and which is also deeply committed not only to the Western alliance, but also to the Western way of life which that alliance exists to defend.

This last is an important point and a major focus of Professor Rustow's important study. An alliance is far more valuable and effective when it is based not only on perceived common interests, important as these may be, but on genuine affinities—a community of beliefs and values, particularly concerning social, political, cultural, and economic matters. Few countries in the Middle East can claim such a relationship with the Western world. The Turkish alignment with the West is not limited to strategic and diplomatic considerations. It is the outward expression of a profound internal change extending over a century-and-a-half of Turkish history, and resulting from a determined and sustained attempt to endow the Turkish people with those freedoms, economic, political, and intellectual, which represent the best that our Western societies have to offer. Despite recurring crises at home, despite several military interventions, Turkey has retained her commitment to democratic values, and each of the military regimes has, of its own free will, given way to a restoration of constitutional and parliamentary government. The road back to freedom is hard and beset with many difficulties, but the intention as well as the overall direction are clear and are firmly maintained. This means that our relationship with Turkey can be a genuine alliance and not, as with some other countries under autocratic rulers, a temporary accommodation which will last only as long as the ruler survives, does not take fright, and does not change his mind.

In Turkey, as in every other country, the prime purpose of foreign policy is the protection and furtherance of national interests, foremost among them the defense of national integrity and sovereignty. Turkey is an old state, and the Turks bring to the consideration of these issues a sharpness of perception and a realism in assessment that are difficult to achieve in newer states with shorter histories and memories. This realism has led, in Turkey, to a policy of alliances which, though sometimes questioned, has hitherto never been seriously challenged, and has survived upheavals and transformations abroad and successive changes of government, and even of regime, at home.

In the foregoing, attention has been given chiefly to Turkey's role as barrier. Professor Rustow, while not underrating the importance of this function, draws our attention to another— that of a cultural and commercial bridge between the West and the Middle East. In recent years, Turkish governments have tried to improve relations with non-Western or even anti-Western groupings—with the Arab world, the Islamic world, more generally with the Third World, and even on some occasions with the non-aligned group. These attempts did not convince the members of the non-aligned bloc to give genuine and full acceptance to the Turks. This comes as no surprise, since in order to become truly convincing, the Turkish government would have had to make changes of a far-reaching, indeed of a structural character—not only in Turkish foreign policy, but also in the political system and orientation of which that foreign policy is the expression.

Of rather more importance are Turkey's relations with the Arab and other Islamic countries. Based on old historical, cultural, and religious ties, these have in recent years been underpinned by a growing economic relationship, through the export of Turkish goods and services to Middle Eastern countries, and the growth of Arab investment in Turkey. Turkish relations with these countries, though not without problems, are friendlier and far more extensive than they have been at any time since the Turkish War of Independence. A notable change has been in Turkish involvement with the Islamic bloc. In earlier days, the secularist principles of the Kemalist Republic precluded any form of interest by the Turkish state in international Islamic activities. In recent years, Turkish participation has grown from the first step of sending observers to active participation at head of state level and playing host to inter-Islamic conferences and meetings.

The combination of an Islamic relationship and a Western alignment is not easy—less for international than for internal reasons. Between the Islamic and Western worlds there is no real conflict of interest, and friendly relations, at least of a bilateral character, exist at various levels. But the pro-Islamic and pro-Western elements inside Turkey draw on different philosophies, with different diagnoses of the Turkish predicament and different prescriptions for its resolution. There are Turks, however, including some in high places, who have found a way to reconcile their religious traditions and their political aspirations, their attachment to their past and their aspirations for the future.

Professor Rustow's book is especially timely in view of the upcoming 1988 national elections, whose outcome will determine Turkey's course for many years to come. Twice before, in the course of their long history, the Turks have set an example and served as a model for others—under the Ottomans, of militant Islam, under Kemal Atatürk, of secular patriotism. If they succeed in their present endeavor to create, without loss of character and identity, a liberal economy, an open society, and a democratic polity, they may once again serve as a model to many other peoples.

Bernard Lewis
*Cleveland E. Dodge Professor
of Near Eastern Studies Emeritus,
Princeton University*

Preface

Turkey has been a crucial test of our containment policy since the Truman Doctrine, an essential link between our European and Middle Eastern strategies, and one of the Third World nations making impressive strides toward economic development and political democracy. This study was prompted by the recognition that even otherwise well-informed Americans tend to know less about Turkey than they do about any country of comparable significance.

This book grew out of a Study Group on Turkey which met at the Council on Foreign Relations between January and December 1984. I am grateful to Peter Grose, then the Council's Director of Middle East Studies, for encouragement in the planning of the group's program; to Ambassador Parker T. Hart for his chairmanship of the group; and to the discussion leaders, commentators, and other study group members for their contributions to the dicussion. Jonathan A. Chanis was the group's rapporteur.

For their critical and helpful comments on an early draft of the manuscript, I am particularly grateful to George Gruen, George S. Harris, Paul Jabber, Nicholas S. Ludington, George L. Sherry, Philip Stoddard, and Nur Yalman. Later drafts elicited valuable suggestions from Nermin Abadan-Unat, John C. Campbell, William M. Hale, and Bernard Lewis. Throughout the writing phase of the project, Paul H. Kreisberg, Director of Studies at the Council, was unfailing in his advice and helpful criticism. In the final stages, it was a distinct pleasure to work with David Kellogg, the Council's Director of Publications, and with May Wu and Steven Monde on his staff.

It also is a pleasure to acknowledge the cheerful and indefatigable help of Council Librarian Janet Rigney and her staff throughout the research phase. Giuseppe Ammendola and Sally Covington, my students at the City University Graduate School, provided research assistance.

The study was supported by a grant from the Ford Foundation. I would also like to express my appreciation to the Institute of Turkish Studies in Washington, D.C., and its director Dr. Heath W. Lowry, for a personal grant. This grant enabled me to travel to Turkey to conduct an extensive series of interviews with government and past and future opposition leaders early in 1984, as the country was taking its crucial steps from military intervention back toward democracy. I am greatly obliged to Prime Minister Turgut Özal and to former premiers Süleyman Demirel and Bülent Ecevit for the privilege of extensive off-the-record interviews. During my visits to Ankara and Istanbul, I vastly benefited from detailed and frank discussions with Bülent Akarcalı, Muammer Aksoy, Türkân Arıkan, Deniz Baykal, Mehmet Ali Birand, İhsan Sabri Çağlayangil, İhsan Doğramacı, Üstün Ergüder, Turhan Feyzioğlu, İsmet Giritli, Emre Gönensay, Metin Heper, Erdal İnönü, Mehmet Keçeciler, Altemur Kılıç, Daniel O. Newberry, Gündüz Ökcun, Osman Okyar, Ergun Özbudun, E. İhsan Özol, Ekrem Pakdemirli, Haydar Saltık, Bahri Savcı, Mümtaz Soysal, Seyfi Taşhan, Neclâ Tekinel, Necip Torumtay, İlter Türkmen, Vakur Versan, and Nilûfer and Aydın Yalçın. For help in arranging contacts, I am indebted to Ambassadors Şükrü Elekdağ in Washington, D.C., and Robert Strausz-Hupe in Ankara; and for contacts and generous hospitality, to Nermin and İlhan Unat in Ankara and Binnaz and Zafer Toprak in Istanbul. Back in New York, my friend Talât Sait Halman gave valued advice and encouragement at every stage of the project.

My wife, Margrit Wreschner Rustow steadfastly and generously bore with me throughout the trials and tribulations of authorship.

Needless to say, I alone take responsibility for the views and judgments expressed in the chapters that follow.

Members of the Study Group were:

Parker T. Hart, *Chairman*	Heath Lowry
Bela Balassa	Nicholas S. Ludington
Cyril E. Black	William B. Macomber
Richard M. Bliss	Marie Antoinette Manca
William P. Bundy	Daniel C. Matuszewski
Jonathan Chanis	Karl E. Meyer
Col. David K. Cooper	John Mroz
Asim Erdilek	Paula R. Newberg
Col. K. Scott Fisher	Matthew Nimetz
Emre Gönensay	Alfred Ogden
Peter Grose	Ergun Özbudun
George Gruen	Col. John G. Pappageorge
Talât Halman	Daniel Pipes
George Harris	Charles Reis
Paul B. Henze	George L. Sherry
James B. Hurlock	James W. Spain
Zalmay Khalilzad	Ronald I. Spiers
Gen. William A. Knowlton	Philip Stoddard
Paul H. Kreisberg	İlter Türkmen
Bruce Kuniholm	Rodney B. Wagner
Ellen Laipson	Walter Weiker
Stephen Larrabee	Albert Wohlstetter
James G. Leonard	Nur Yalman
Bernard Lewis	Frank G. Zarb
David H. Lowenfeld	Adm. Elmo R. Zumwalt, Jr.

Dankwart A. Rustow

New York
February 1987

Turkish Spelling and Pronunciation

Most letters in Turkish are pronounced as in English, with the
following exceptions:

c: as j or dg in "judge"

ç: as ch in "charm"

ğ: lengthens the preceding vowel; or, between vowels, serves
as a glide—as w in "snowing" or y in "saying"

İ, i: as i in "is"

I, ı: as in "will"

ö: as in German "schön" or French eu in "heureux"

ş: as sh in "shop"

ü: as in German "über" or French u in "une"

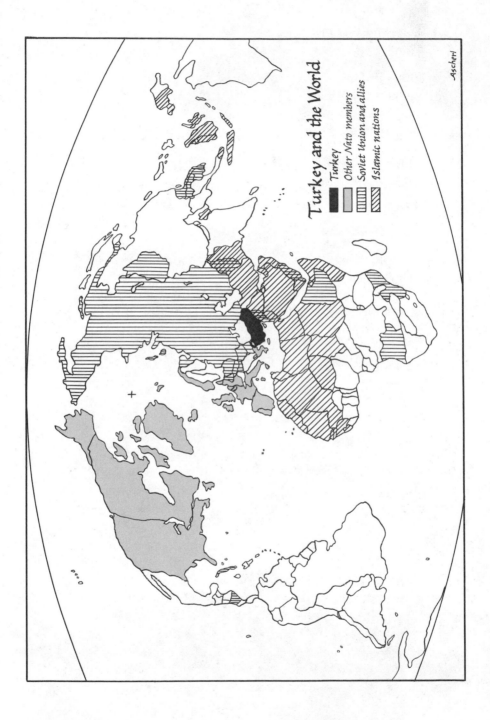

Turkey and the World

Turkey
Other Nato members
Soviet Union and allies
Islamic nations

Ascher

One

Bridge over the Bosporus: Turkey in the 1980s

Bridge for Sale

One day in 1984, Prime Minister Turgut Özal of Turkey announced his government's decision to sell bonds for the bridge over the Bosporus, with toll revenues to be earmarked to pay interest and amortization. The sale fulfilled a promise made in the whirlwind election campaign which late in 1983 had given Özal's newly founded Motherland Party one of the largest parliamentary majorities in the checkered history of Turkish democracy.

The bond sale, in the contemporary Turkish context, was symbolic and controversial. It expressed Turgut Özal's commitment to private enterprise as the path to Turkey's economic future, an ideological position as firm and outspoken as that of Ronald Reagan, Margaret Thatcher, or any Western economist of the liberal school. Yet Özal in private life was an observant Muslim and onetime pilgrim to Mecca, and among the Turkish businessmen who supported him most enthusiastically were those who in recent years had landed billions of dollars of construction contracts in Saudi Arabia, Libya, and other Arab countries. Özal's first address to the Ankara parliament in 1983 had suggested that the whole of Turkey was "a natural bridge between the West and the Middle East."

Putting the Bosporus Bridge "on the block" also reflected Özal's flair for publicity. The law under which his government issued the bridge bonds had envisaged the sale of the entire vast network of Turkey's "state economic enterprises." But to

1

the Turkish news media and their audiences, that legislation at once became known as the "Bridge Sale Law." Among all those government properties, the Bosporus Bridge was by far the most profitable: there was little question that its bonds would be sold long before private shareholders could be lined up to invest in Turkey's hydroelectric dams, railways, steel mills, cigarette plants, or international and domestic air services.

The Bosporus Bridge had long since become a source of intense pride to residents of Istanbul and to the Turkish public at large. To Özal's critics, the bridge sale seemed a willful and ostentatious squandering of national patrimony—a reversal of policy as shocking as the forced substitution two generations earlier of the European hat for the traditional fez and turban.

When the 3,500-foot span had first been opened in the fall of 1973, it was the world's longest suspension bridge outside the United States, and in the following decade it attracted a mounting volume of traffic. There were the daily commuters and commercial deliveries within Istanbul, Turkey's largest city and chief banking and trading center, with its busy harbor and its then three million inhabitants on the European and Asian shores of the Bosporus waterway. There was the growing stream of long-distance trucks plying the route between Western Europe and Turkey, and beyond to the Middle East; and that traffic had vastly grown in the 1980s, as the protracted Iraq-Iran war in the Persian Gulf made both countries dependent on alternative trade routes overland. Within a few years of its opening, the tolls of the Bosporus Bridge had repaid its construction cost. By the mid-1980s Istanbul's own population had grown to over five million, and severe traffic jams during the morning and evening rush hours were an almost daily ordeal. After completing the bond sale for the first Bosporus Bridge in 1984, the Özal government therefore made plans for the construction of a second, parallel span.

Turgut Özal had won his 1983 election with an economic reform program amounting to a free-enterprise revolution, and few people symbolized the fast-changing Turkish scene as vividly as did the new prime minister himself. Trained as an engineer in Turkey and the United States, Özal in his earlier career had been associated with large public works projects such as the Keban Dam on the Euphrates in southeastern Turkey and the bridge now for sale. Later he had risen through the ranks of the State Planning Organization, run unsuccessfully on the Islamic-conservative National Salvation Party's ticket in 1977, and by 1979 emerged as the chief economic adviser to Prime Minister Süleyman Demirel at the time of Turkey's debt renegotiations with the International Monetary Fund. It thus had been Özal who developed the austerity and devaluation plan which in 1980 turned Turkey around from its earlier debt crisis. Indeed, so crucial was Özal's part in the delicate negotiations with Turkey's foreign creditors that the government of General Kenan Evren, installed by a military coup in September 1980, not only retained Özal's services but promoted him to deputy prime minister in charge of economic affairs.

In this new role as chief economic policy maker in 1980–82, Özal was instrumental in the quest of Turkish construction firms for new markets in Libya, Saudi Arabia, and other Middle Eastern countries. No prior government in Ankara would have taken such pride in selling revenues from a major monument of public construction like the Bosporus Bridge to private investors, and no other public figure was as closely identified with the economic transformation that generated a growing volume of traffic through its toll gates.

Predictably, Özal's efforts to restructure the Turkish economy ran into opposition from entrenched economic interests—which breathed a sigh of relief when the Evren junta in 1982 decided to replace him as its chief economic policy maker. And it was that earlier dismissal which in part prompted Özal to challenge the junta's own spoon-fed parties in the 1983 elections.

Crisis and Recovery

The debt crisis which launched Turgut Özal on his political career represented the latest turn in a cycle of instability characteristic of rapidly growing economies—and also of precarious democracies, as witness the recent (and far more serious) debt crises of Mexico, Argentina, Brazil, and many others. In Turkey, the 1950s, 1960s, and 1970s began as periods of prosperity and rapid agricultural and then industrial development; yet each decade ended in a crisis of inflation, unmanageable foreign debt, and domestic tension, punctuated by growing violence and intervals of military intervention and repression (1960–61, 1971–73, 1980–83).

Contradictory indications continued into the 1980s. General Kenan Evren and his military colleagues, by their September 1980 coup, restored law and order—and surprised their critics by proceeding with impartial vigor against ultranationalist groups on the right as well as Marxists and anarchists on the left.

The further results of the generals' intervention, however, remained highly controversial. A year after the coup, the junta convened a consultative assembly to draft a democratic constitution; and this new basic law was confirmed by a 1982 referendum, which also elected General Evren to a seven-year presidential term—unopposed. Before scheduling the parliamentary elections of 1983, the Evren junta carefully excluded the political parties and the most popular leaders of the preceding period, prompting the European Parliament to reject the result as undemocratic. Yet Özal's last-minute entry into the 1983 race and the clear victory of his Motherland Party obviously upset the generals' carefully laid plans for some sort of "controlled" democracy.

The immediate effect resembled that of an automobile with dual controls and on a zigzag course. Whereas President Evren and his advisers concentrated on matters of national security, Prime Minister Özal assumed full charge of economic policy at home and abroad. Yet the question of how far or how soon Turkey would return toward democracy remained in suspense for some time—except as the cumulative drift of events forced the pace. Initially Özal and his followers welcomed the decision to hold local and provincial elections as early as March 1984, and in a campaign to which some of the previously banned political parties were readmitted, saw their electoral majority reconfirmed. In mid-1984, President Evren bitterly denounced as "traitors" a group of intellectuals who had petitioned for restoration of full freedom of speech and press; yet Özal saw to it that the petition was published despite continuing martial law restrictions on the press.

Progress toward observance of human rights similarly remained uneven. Before the coup, terrorism and violence between armed leftist and rightist groups had taken a staggering toll of more than twenty lives a day. Yet the terrorists, suspects, and political dissidents arrested in the massive roundups following the 1980 coup were often subjected to inhuman torture, as were Kurdish separatists rounded up in the mid-1980s. Meanwhile, largely in response to criticism from Western Europe, Turkish authorities began to discipline or prosecute police officers accused of brutality toward prisoners—prompting the European Human Rights Commission to drop a case against Turkey that had been pending since 1982. Still, human rights organizations such as Amnesty International and Helsinki Watch documented continuing maltreatment of prisoners. In 1986, "[t]he human rights situation in Turkey remain[ed] in a state of flux and contradiction. . .[although] that very ferment" was seen to be "the best reason for hope."[1]

Late in 1985, martial law was lifted in the major cities and throughout most of Turkey, the press enjoyed wide freedom, and even the political parties of the 1970s reemerged under new labels and nominally changed leadership. By then, however, Özal's own attitude seemed somewhat ambiguous. He had encouraged many of the crucial steps toward democracy; yet, as criticism of his economic policies mounted and public opinion polls began to go against him, Özal's Motherland Party could not help benefiting from the continued presence in parliament of the weak parties improvised in 1983 at the Evren junta's behest.

Whatever Özal's own political future, there was hope that Turkish political parties would be both more responsive to popular wishes and more responsible in conducting the government than those of the past. The electoral law of 1982 had abandoned the extreme version of proportional representation which in the 1970s had led to party splintering, uneasy cabinet coalitions, and continual parliamentary deadlocks. In its third democratic experiment, Turkey in the 1980s seems headed for a solid two-party system, with the small Marxist, ultranationalist, and Islamic-extremist minorities henceforth reduced to parliamentary insignificance. Indeed, the provisions of the electoral law favoring the established major parties were further reinforced in 1986. With the major arms-smuggling networks and arms caches rooted out by the 1980–83 military regime, there is every indication that Turkey has overcome the intense violence of the 1970s.

Still, it is obvious that Turkey's political debate will grow livelier with the approach of the national elections in 1988. By 1985 the consolidation of the opposition on the left was virtually complete, except for some continued jockeying for leadership. In the Ankara parliament, occasional party shifts slightly increased the initial majority of Özal and his Motherland Party. And in September 1986, the results of a partial by-election, although having little immediate effect in parliament, buoyed the hopes of ex-premier Süleyman Demirel and his followers of displacing Özal in the 1988 elections if not before.

In sum, while Turkey in the mid-1980s is clearly moving toward democracy, ultimate judgments on the country's ability to combine democratic freedom, rapid economic growth, and public order will have to await the outcome of future elections and governmental successions.

Özal's own electoral fortunes will obviously depend on the performance of the economy. Inflation has come down from its earlier triple-digit figures, but is still far above the 25 percent level that Özal had promised in the 1983 campaign. Turkey's growing export industry remains enthusiastic in its support of Özal; yet his efforts to dismantle the entrenched structures of tariffs and subsidies have antagonized many of the older, well-established economic forces; and among the urban middle and working classes, high unemployment and continuing inflation have contributed to lingering dissatisfaction.

Turkey's major economic asset, no doubt, is its hardworking people. The substantial remittances from Turkish workers in

Western Europe since the 1960s and from contractors and workers in the Middle East since the 1970s have provided a steady inflow of foreign exchange, at times exceeding the earnings from all of Turkey's exports. More generally, in its foreign economic relations, Özal's Turkey has made great strides in extricating itself from the payments crisis of the late 1970s. With the lifting of restrictions on foreign investment, major American banks have opened new branch offices in Istanbul, and Arab oil magnates have purchased villas on the Bosporus. Still, such indications of recovery remain inconclusive for the future: the bulk of the rescheduled debt payments is due only in the late 1980s; and foreign industrial investors are naturally slower to arrive than bank managers and villa-buying sheiks.

Even if the soundness of Özal's overall strategy is granted, there remain many dangers along the way. An export-oriented country would escape its age-old insulation from the world economy and raise standards of performance by maximizing its contribution to the global division of labor. Yet it would also be fully exposed to forces beyond it's control, notably the ebb and flow of international business cycles, and competition for export markets from other newly industrializing nations, such as South Korea, Taiwan, Brazil, and Israel.

Thus, in recent decades, the export of manual workers to West Germany and of construction crews to Arab countries creatively made use of what economists would call Turkey's "comparative advantage." Nonetheless, the flow of Turkish workers abroad slowed down as Europe faced a major recession in consequence of the OPEC oil shocks of the 1970s; and conversely the boom for Turkish contracting firms in the Middle East was slowed down by the sharp decline in the revenues of oil-exporting countries in the 1980s.

Similarly, in the domestic economy, any major shift of policy, such as Özal's espousal of liberalism over state enterprise, involves painful adjustments over the short term, as existing structures of protection and subsidy are dismantled—and rewards only over the longer term, as the changing economic climate encourages new investments and those investments bear fruit. In sum, Özal's ideal of Turkey as a future Japan of the Middle East, committed to ancestral values and up-to-date international technology, however attractive its historic and long-term logic, remains at best a somewhat distant vision. Meanwhile, the question remains whether Özal's political program and Turkey's economy can stay the course.

Despite mounting criticism at home, Özal's popularity in international financial circles and his flair for publicity continued undiminished. Soon after the bond sale for the first Bosporus Bridge, his government proudly announced the award of the contract for the second bridge to a Japanese-Turkish consortium of construction companies; and before long a major American bank was boasting of its success in putting together the necessary half-billion dollars' worth of long-term financing.[2] In 1986, Turkey had the satisfaction of surpassing Japan as the OECD country headed for the highest economic growth rate for the year.

A New Start for Ankara and Washington

In contrast to some of the short-term economic difficulties, Turkey's foreign relations of the 1980s registered some immediate successes. Notably, the Defense and Economic Cooperation Agreement (DECA) between Ankara and Washington in March 1980 restored relations with Turkey's main Western ally to their old cordiality.

When the first Bosporus Bridge was built in the late 1960s, the Ankara government had officially called it the "Bridge of Europe"; and West Germany's foreign minister, Willy Brandt, had declared that its construction "signifies Turkey's wish to join Europe." That wish to join the West, indeed, had long been apparent. In the late 1940s and 1950s Turkey had entered its strategic alliance with the United States and associated itself with the early movement toward Western European unity. The Truman Doctrine spelled out for Greece and Turkey what became America's global policy of containing Soviet expansion. In quick succession (1947–52), the Ankara government joined the Marshall Plan, the Council of Europe, and the Atlantic

Alliance. By 1964 Turkey had become an associate member of Europe's Common Market, and in the next decade nearly two million Turkish workers and their families took advantage of the employment opportunities thus opened to them in Germany and elsewhere in Western Europe.

Turkey's leaders had eagerly sought those multiple Western ties as strategic protection from Russia's aggressive designs and also as a welcome source of funds for economic growth. But to Turkey's political elite at midcentury, those expanding Western and European associations conveyed a message of even deeper meaning. Since the founding of the Turkish Republic in the 1920s, indeed ever since the decline of the Ottoman sultans, Turkey had moved from its traditional Islamic and Middle Eastern ways toward the ideal of a modern, Westernized nation-state. Now, with Turkey a full member of NATO and an associate of the European Community, the goal at long last seemed in sight.

In the 1960s and 1970s, however, a number of severe strains entered into Turkey's Western relations. A smouldering dispute with Greece over Cyprus, and later over air and sea rights in the Aegean, brought the two southeastern NATO allies to the verge of war and caused recurrent tensions between Washington and Ankara. In 1964, President Lyndon Johnson kept Turkey from invading Cyprus by the blunt threat of reconsidering NATO's "obligation to protect Turkey against the Soviet Union."[3] A decade later, the U.S. Congress responded to Turkey's two-phase invasion of the island by suspending bilateral military aid. By the late 1970s, the Ankara government itself began to expand its relations outside the Western bloc, accepting substantial amounts of Soviet economic aid, joining the Islamic Conference Organization, and establishing closer economic ties with countries such as Iraq, Libya, Saudi Arabia, and Iran.

Understandably, there was concern in Washington that Turkey's closer diplomatic and economic ties with Moscow and its own Middle Eastern neighbors would weaken its crucial position in the Western alliance. In the short run, those fears proved unfounded, as continuing cooperation between the ex-

ecutive branch in Washington and successive Turkish governments limited the damage of the arms embargo that Congress
had temporarily imposed on Turkey.

In the longer run, Turkish-American relations are likely to
face two recurrent difficulties. First, Turkey's northeastern
frontier remains one of the few points where Soviet expansionism has remained contained in its original borders of 1921; and
this very success of the U.S.-Turkish alliance may tempt each
partner to take the other for granted. Second, for Ankara, the
American alliance has been its most vital international link; for
the United States, it is only one in a complex network of global
relations. For Turkish citizens, whatever their particular status
or attitude, American civilization remains a powerful and
closely felt presence. By contrast, few Americans have any
clear ideas of Turkey, and those they hold include numerous
stereotypes drawn from sources such as *The Abduction from the
Seraglio*, historic Greek and Armenian grievances, media re-
ports on Turkey's intense bout of political violence and repression in the late 1970s and early 1980s, and the many TV reruns
of *Midnight Express* (a 1978 movie depicting the torture inflicted
on an American drug-smuggler in a Turkish jail).

Considering the crucial role Turkey plays in our global strategy, even educated Americans tend to know less about Turkey
than they do about any country of comparable importance.
This book hopes to reduce this information gap by presenting a
sketch of the Western and Islamic elements in today's Turkish
society (Chapter 2), followed by an assessment of Turkey's
economic development (Chapter 3) and the problems and prospects of its progress toward democracy (Chapter 4). An exami-
nation of the elements of change and continuity in Turkish
foreign policy and of past tensions between Ankara and Washington (Chapter 5) will lead, in conclusion, to an evaluation of
Turkey's place in America's foreign policy (Chapter 6).

Whither Turkey?

The success of the Bosporus Bridge as a road link can be measured accurately enough by toll revenues, traffic jams, and

bond sales. The bold concept of Turkey itself as "natural bridge" between the West and the Middle East remains to be tested by social and economic trends and by political events in the future. In the chapters that follow, a review of recent cultural, economic, and domestic-political developments will enable us to examine, in their context, some of the questions that will preoccupy policy analysts in the years ahead—questions that are posed by Turkey's very location at the crossroads between Western Europe, the Soviet Union, and the Middle East.

Will the current radical free-trade policies enable Turkey to ride the crest of the economic tides in the world at large? Or will they produce an economy helplessly exposed to cyclical depressions in the West and to falling oil prices in the Middle East? In Turkey itself, will free enterprise open up such opportunities for economic betterment and social ascent as to guarantee its own political momentum—or will population pressures, stock market crashes, or a growing cleavage between rich and poor set off an irresistible clamor for social security, price controls, and other forms of state intervention?

How viable is the combination of free-enterprise economics, democratic politics, and private religious observance represented by leaders such as Özal or Demirel as a model for Turkey's next generation? Or is there any danger that this moderate and liberal synthesis will be ground down in a surge of economic frustration, Islamic fundamentalism, violence between left and right, and military repression?

By 1986 Özal had made Turkey's future membership in the European Community a central theme of his foreign policy pronouncements. Yet how realistic is this prospect in view of the wide gap in living standards between Western Europe and Turkey and of the unresolved political problems with Greece? On Turkey's Asian frontiers, the Middle Eastern scene of the late 1980s and 1990s remains full of risks—an Iranian victory over Iraq or, on the contrary, a collapse of Iran in the post-Khomeini period; further confrontations between the United States and radical forces, as earlier in Lebanon or Libya; or a renewed sharpening of the Arab-Israeli conflict. What will be Ankara's reaction to such future contingencies? Specifically, is there any danger that Turkey might falter in its crucial role as a barrier to Soviet penetration of the Middle Eastern and the Mediterranean regions?

Or could Turkey's geographic role as a bridge to the Middle East conversely acquire a dynamic political dimension in the future? Specifically, might Turkey's rapid industrialization serve as a stimulus to regional prosperity regardless of the vagaries of the price of oil? Might Ankara's example of even-handed neutrality in the Iraq-Iran war and improving relations with Israel help lower the temperature of regional conflict generally, or even contribute to that "strategic consensus" that proved so elusive to Secretary of State Alexander M. Haig in the first Reagan administration?

In sum, is there any danger that the country's new economic ties to the Middle East might weaken Turkey's cultural commitment to the West and strategic ties with NATO and the United States? Or are Turkey's manifold and growing connections sound and firm enough to help bridge the gap that, politically and economically, has so long separated the Middle East from the West?

Two

"...We Go to the West": A Society on the Move

Thorns and Roses

The Turkish scene on a first visit may impress the foreigner with its diversity: squealing oxcarts in the villages and Ankara's dense traffic jams and smog; elegant villas on the Bosporus and shantytowns in the nearby hills; the society hostess in her Parisian gown, urban teenagers in their blue jeans, and the ubiquitous head scarves of the poorer women; blaring, American-style rock music and the Arabic prayer call resounding from the tops of the minarets five times a day.

Differences in Turkish society of status, education, and wealth, and differences between Middle Eastern-Islamic and modern Western customs are closely interrelated; together they form an open and highly dynamic pattern. The very presence of the shantytown dweller and his frequent visits to his native village bring a touch of rural life to the city. The afternoon prayer call from the urban minaret is likely to have been taped and electronically amplified. And an attitude of mutual tolerance allows a minority to respond by interrupting work for quiet prayer in a corner—and most people to continue their nonreligious routines, such as the predinner shopping of the working-class wife or the cocktail party of the high social set.

The major social divide is marked not by hereditary status or income but by education—always a central concern of Turkish government and, in the past century and a half, a powerful force for Westernization and then for social equality. The Ottoman Empire in its classical days (ca. 1450 to 1800) was centered around a set of schools near the sultan's palace. In those palace schools, sons of Balkan peasants or Caucasus slaves were trained as officers and administrators, sent to the frontiers, and recalled to Istanbul, where they might rise to the rank of pasha or vezir. Similarly, the learned hierarchy of Islamic ulema—imams and hatibs (prayer leaders and mosque orators), muftis and kadis—had their own network of schools throughout the Ottoman realm, with students drawn mostly from the small towns in Turkish Anatolia and the Arab countries.

"We come from the East, we go to the West," says a proverb that recalls the original Turkish migration from Central Asia to Anatolia in the eleventh century. That westward move continued as the Ottoman Turks conquered their empire from Yemen to Hungary and from the Caucasus to Algeria—the largest and most durable realm west of China since the fall of Rome. Later, the Ottomans' failure at the second siege of Vienna initiated a long phase of defeat and withdrawal (1683–1918). After much soul-searching, the sultans' response to this imposed eastward retreat was to start going west in novel ways: for the art of printing and the latest techniques of artillery and naval warfare; for a system of military training, first with instructors called from Europe and then with Ottoman students sent abroad; for more comprehensive taxation and conscription; for the instructional methods of French *lycées* and a parliamentary constitution adapted from Belgium; and for Prussian officers to reorganize the Ottoman general staff. This policy of Westernization was maintained in the face of further military defeats, of lamentations by the ulema, and a widening gap between traditional Islamic and new Western elements in Ottoman law and education.

Understandably, the final Ottoman defeats in the Balkan and First World wars (1912–18) exacerbated the argument between traditionalists and Westernizers. In 1913, an Istanbul journalist succinctly stated the position of the radical reformers: "There is no second civilization; civilization means European civilization, and it must be imported with both its roses and its thorns."[1]

This, in effect, became the policy of Kemal Atatürk, who

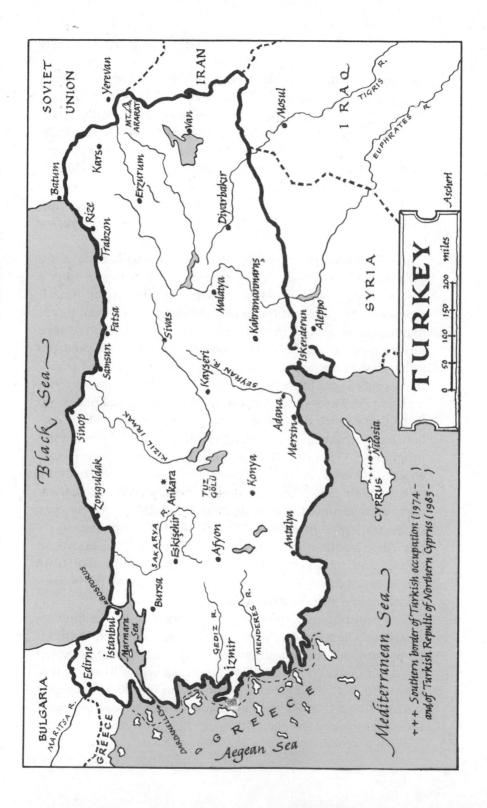

TURKEY

miles
0 50 100 150 200

+++ Southern border of Turkish occupation (1974—)
and of Turkish Republic of Northern Cyprus (1983—)

SOVIET UNION

• Yerevan

IRAN

MT. ARARAT

• Van

• Kars

• Erzurum

Diyarbakır

Mosul

IRAQ

TIGRIS R.

EUPHRATES R.

Batum

Rize

Trabzon

Fatsa

Sivas

Malatya

Kahramanmaraş

İskenderun

Aleppo

SYRIA

Ascher

Black Sea

Samsun

Sinop

Zonguldak

KIZIL IRMAK

Kayseri

SEYHAN R.

Adana

Mersin

Konya

Antalya

TUZ GÖLÜ

SAKARYA R. Ankara

Eskişehir

Afyon

Bursa

İstanbul

BOSPORUS

Marmara Sea

Edirne

MARITSA R.

BULGARIA

GREECE

DARDANELLES

GEDIZ R.

İzmir

MENDERES R.

Aegean Sea

Mediterranean Sea

CYPRUS

Nicosia

GREECE

founded a modern nation-state on the ruins of the Ottoman
Empire, and deposed the sultan to become the first president of
the Republic of Turkey (1923–38). Following the defeat of 1918,
Atatürk, with equal determination, rejected past Ottoman imperial claims as well as the current designs of European powers
to absorb Turkey into their own empires. Specifically, he appealed to the nation, from the highest government official to
the lowliest peasant, to defend its homeland against invading
Greek armies bent on incorporating Anatolia into a Greater
Greece.

This Greek-Turkish war of 1919–23, known to Turks as their
"War of Independence," might be considered this century's
first successful war of national liberation; and at the time it
aroused strong admiration among subject peoples from Egypt
to India engaged in their own uneven struggle against Western
imperialism. Turkey's war, however, was one to preserve
rather than attain political independence—and it came to mark
the turning point in the ruling elite's transition from an Otto-
man-imperial to a Turkish-national consciousness. Fresh from
its battlefield victories, the Turkish people abandoned the earlier, hesitant pace of reform to embrace Atatürk's sweeping
program of Westernization—and did so from a sense of free
choice, not of duress. That program, which might truly be
called a cultural revolution, brought, in rapid order, seculariza-
tion of government and education (1924–25), European law
codes and styles of dress (1925–27), the Latin alphabet to replace the traditional Arabic-Islamic script (1928),[2] European
theater and music, and a Western educational system from
elementary schools to the universities, with many of the professors at first recruited from Europe.[3]

Two centuries ago, the sultans' military and government officials had started going west for their textbooks and training.
Since the 1930s, the rapidly expanding school system devised
by Atatürk has allowed the population as a whole to join in that
westward trek. And whereas France and Germany provided
the chief models of Western education down to Atatürk's day,
recent reforms have been patterned mostly on American educational practice.

Education: The Ladder to the Top

In Turkey's steeply graded class structure, education has always been the chief avenue of mobility, the stair or escalator by which the son or grandson of a simple peasant can make it to the top—whether to the rank of vezir or pasha in Ottoman days or of company executive or cabinet minister in our own. Atatürk emphasized the equal-opportunity function of education by supplementing the system of *lycées* and universities, which had long drawn aspiring youngsters to the towns, with a system of "village institutes" that would respond more directly to rural educational needs.

In the 1950s, the U.S. foreign aid program, with its emphasis on irrigation, crop rotation, and farm mechanization, accelerated that same rural transformation—as did the transition, since the late 1940s, from Atatürk's authoritarian single-party system to electoral competition among several political parties. Among the tangible benefits of democracy that peasant voters soon came to expect were better roads to bring their produce to market, and village schools to educate their children. Toward the end of Atatürk's rule, in 1935, only one Turkish child in three was going to primary school; today the ratio is more than nine out of ten. In 1950, only one-third of the Turkish population was literate; by 1980, in a population more than doubled in thirty years, the literacy rate had risen to 69 percent—with a majority of the women and as many as four out of five men now able to read and write. In view of such rapidly increasing school attendance, virtually the entire population is sure to become literate by the turn of the century.

There has been a corresponding expansion at all levels of education. Between 1960 and 1975, the number of *lycée* (junior college) graduates in the population quadrupled, and that of graduates of universities and technical schools tripled. More Turkish citizens are pursuing college studies today than were going to elementary school in the early years of the Republic. By the 1970s, there were teachers' training institutes in all but one of Turkey's sixty-seven provinces; and the reform of higher education since 1980 was designed in part to break up the concentration of universities and technical schools in Istanbul and Ankara, and thus bring higher education closer to the rural people of Anatolia.

By opening the gates of advancement ever more widely, education is becoming a powerful force not just for ascent but for social equality. Once you have entered a *lycée*, a technical school, or a university, it matters little whether you were sent there on your parents' income, on the savings remitted by relatives working in Germany, or on one of the many government scholarship programs. As a perceptive American noted a generation ago, "Children of the rich and the poor, children of cabinet ministers and of gatekeepers are classmates in the schools."[4]

A system of competitive examinations provides access to Turkey's distinctive elite schools, many of which go back to the midnineteenth-century era of Ottoman reform. There is the Lycée de Galatasaray, with its French-Turkish curriculum and its tradition of alumni in the diplomatic corps. There is Robert College, an American-Turkish high school founded by American missionaries in the 1850s, which today is training many of Turkey's new business class. There is the University of the Bosporus, formerly the higher education branch of Robert College and now a state university with an English-language curriculum and separate graduate divisions, including business and engineering. There are the Harbiye (or officers' training school) and the Mülkiye (or civil service school) of Ottoman days, both in due course moved from Istanbul to Ankara to become, respectively, the War Academy and the Faculty of Political Science of Ankara University. Other elite institutions, such as the Middle East Technical University and Hacettepe University in Ankara, whose curricula are also in English, are of more recent origin, dating back to the 1950s.

One major benefit of a diploma from one of these elite schools is the network of contacts it provides in government, the professions, or more recently, business. Former classmates form friendships as durable as family ties, and teachers are revered by their former students for life—two further indications of the high value Turkish society places on education.

Meanwhile, the program of sending Turkish students abroad, which began on a small scale in late Ottoman and early Republican days, has been vastly expanded, most recently as a result of American foreign aid and corresponding efforts of the Turkish government. A majority of members of Turkey's parliament, or Grand National Assembly, by now claim a knowledge of one or more foreign languages, with English in recent decades taking the lead over French and German. Aside from some self-made entrepreneurs, few Turkish citizens can expect to rise to the top in a university, government, the professions, or business without having received part of their training in Europe or the United States.

Of recent Turkish prime ministers, Süleyman Demirel was an Eisenhower Fellow in the United States; Bülent Ecevit, a Robert College graduate, worked in the Turkish press attaché's office in London and received a postgraduate fellowship at Harvard; Admiral Bülend Ulusu held an assignment with the NATO Mediterranean forces; and Turgut Özal spent a year working at the World Bank in Washington. The Social Democratic Party, which in 1984 emerged as the major opposition, was founded by Professor Erdal İnönü, a theoretical physicist of international renown who received his training in Istanbul and California to become a faculty member and administrator at two of Turkey's English-language universities.

The purely economic contrasts that education helps to overcome are not as sharp as might be imagined. Turkey, to be sure, has a sizable group of large landowners, including commercial farmers of the western coastal region and the *derebeyis* ("lords of the valley") of the southeast, whose extensive holdings are parceled out among poor sharecroppers. The prevalent rural property, however, is the family farm—the overall pattern of land distribution being less even than in Western Europe, yet far more so than in neighboring Greece, let alone the Arab Middle East. Above all, it is only natural, in view of the tangible social advantages of formal education, that any Turkish village family will try to send its sons—and nowadays also its daughters—to school, provided there is a school available in the village and their labor can be spared around the family farm.

It is the same desire for economic improvement that has lured Turkish villagers by the hundreds of thousands first to the shantytowns around the major cities, and more recently to factory and service jobs in Western Europe.

The Language of Tradition and Modernity

Several generations ago, the difference between upper and lower class was obvious in their habits of speech, but that particular gap is continually narrowing. The Ottoman elite over the centuries accepted Arabic as the authentic tongue of God's revelation to the Prophet Muhammad and also as the language of law and science; and Persian as the language of poetry. As a result, Ottoman Turkish over the centuries became replete with esoteric vocabulary and locutions derived from Arabic and Persian—in sharp contrast to the plain Turkish speech of the simple workman or villager. Indeed, the gentlemen and ladies of Istanbul were proud to think of themselves as "Ottomans," reserving the term "Turk," with evident condescension, for the unlettered peasants and nomads of Anatolia.

Against this background of a society sharply divided by habits of speech, Atatürk's "language revolution" of the 1930s set out to create a Turkish cleansed of Arabic and Persian, and supplemented, where necessary, with words derived from the medieval Turkish dialects of Central Asia. The textbooks for the rapidly expanding school system served as the natural vehicle for propagating this "Pure Turkish" idiom. Some of the new vocabulary at first proved as puzzling as the Arabic words it replaced; yet the main effect was to popularize and simplify the language of the schools at a time when their doors were opened wide to boys and girls of all social classes.

The historic trend may be illustrated by some of the words introduced to designate social or technical innovations. A century ago, these typically followed Arabic patterns: the General Staff School on the Prussian model, introduced by a late sultan, was called *Mekteb-i Erkân-i Harbiye*—three Arabic words with two Persian connectives. Other terms were taken directly from

Italian, French, or other European languages, and among these *posta, tünel* (Istanbul's one-stop subway), *telgraf, vapur* (steamboat), *otel* (hotel), *gazete* (newspaper), *radyo, telefon, üniversite,* and *futbol* (soccer)—and more recently *kokteyl* and *televizyon*—have become fully naturalized. But in the post-Atatürk era, most of the necessary new words are being derived from Turkish roots; thus a computer becomes a *bilgisayar,* or "knowledge counter."

The pace of linguistic change has been hastened by the competition of newspapers, radio, and television for a mass audience. Between 1950 and 1978, the aggregate circulation of Turkish newspapers quadrupled, to 2.5 million, and that of registered radio sets increased twelve times, to 4.3 million. By 1984 the number of television sets had reached 6.3 million, or a nationwide average of three for every four households—far exceeding the number of either radios or newspapers. Among Turkey's most effective political speakers has been Süleyman Demirel, who cultivates a consciously traditional and paternalistic bearing; but also men such as Bülent Ecevit, a poet and journalist with a simple, gripping style in speech and writing; and Turgut Özal with his disarmingly homelike, colloquial manner both on television and with official visitors.

The people of Turkey thus live their lives in a dynamic environment dominated by social and technical innovations adopted from the West, and called either by newly coined Turkish or common international names. Nonetheless, in spheres of life such as family ritual or social courtesy, the traditional patterns persist or smoothly blend with more recent customs—for which a European word may prove eminently appropriate. Thus, in most of Turkish society, the Jewish-Islamic taboo on pork remains universal, except that a fashionable hostess may include cold ham among the hors d'oeuvres served at cocktail time. She will be careful, however, to refer to it as "*jambon*"; for to call it by the plain word "*domuz*" (pig, pork) might make even her most emancipated guests shudder in disgust.

Mustaches for men and head scarves for women remain characteristic of observant Muslims and villagers and townspeople of the lower class. Blue beads (known as the traditional remedy against the "evil eye") decorate automobile rearview mirrors and many small shops. Chewing gum has joined worry beads as a ready antidote to nervousness. The Koran's prohibition on fermented drink has been universally circumvented since Ottoman days by the use of *rakı,* an anise-flavored distilled liquor that has long been Turkey's national drink,[5] or, in fashionable urban society, of vodka or whiskey; whereas Turkey's excellent wines are served only in the most Westernized homes.

Family names, introduced by legal fiat in 1935, are taking hold in daily use, as they help distinguish among the dozens of Mehmets or Fatmas whom geographic and social mobility may bring into contact. But Turks still address each other politely as Mehmet *Bey* or Fatma *Hanım,* with the traditional honorific following the given name; or more deferentially as *Beyefendi* ("Sir") or *Hanımefendi* ("Madam")—reserving the officially prescribed *Bay* and *Bayan* (which precede the name) mostly for mail envelopes or formal documents. *Paşam* ("My pasha") remains the respectful form of address to a general—and a proud, doting mother's phrase of endearment for her boy.

Birthday celebrations, unknown in traditional Islam, have become universal among urban educated Turks. Stationery stores thus carry greeting cards for birthdays and holidays, and even cards with pictures of a friendly man in white beard and red wool suit called "Noel Baba," a translation of Père Noël, the French cousin of Santa Claus—for such cards make a perfect adjunct to the "New Year's present" you may wish to send to your friends' children. Soccer (known as *futbol*) has long since replaced greased wrestling as the national spectator sport; yet the shadow puppet plays about the shrewd Karagöz ("Blackeye") and his pompous companion Hacıvat survive into the age of movies and television. Outdoors, the sidewalk newsstands, with lucrative impartiality and within the tolerant limits of the law, sell pornography, lottery tickets, popular religious tracts, and the many mass-circulation sports, cartoon, and humor magazines.[6]

In their social relations, Turks continue to practice their traditional politeness, with separate "good-bye" formulas used by the person who departs (*Allaha ısmarladık*—"In God's keep-

ing") and the one who stays (*Güle güle*—"Smiling, smiling").
Estağfırullah (Turco-Arabic for "May God forgive *my* sins") remains the standard response to a friend's self-disparagement,
abject apology, or excessive compliment. *Başınız sağ olsun*
("May your head be healthy") is the ritual wish to someone
whose relative or friend has died. *Geçmiş olsun* ("May it be
past!") is the universal formula that wishes away sickness or
discomfort from pneumonia to a mere sneeze (and details of
your own or your friend's health are not taboo as a subject of
conversation). Few Turks will make a statement or promise
about the future without injecting the phrase "*inşallah*" ("if
God wills"). *Allah bağışlasın* ("May God grant") and *Allah göster-
mesin* ("God forbid") remain the automatic incantations by
which welcome and unwelcome events are hastened or
averted.

This elaborate language of courtesy and politeness is practiced at the top of the social scale and emulated by those eager
to rise from below. Together with the tolerant compromises
between religion and secularism and the many avenues of mobility, it provides time-tested emotional insurance against the
changing fortunes of economy and political regimes.

Women in Turkey's Changing Society

The emancipation of Turkish women remains an important test
of social progress. A century ago, foreign schools in Istanbul
and Izmir were the only ones to admit girls, and in 1901, Halide
Edib was the first young Muslim to graduate from the women's
branch of Robert College in Istanbul. After the Ottoman defeat
in World War I, she attracted attention by her rousing speeches
for national independence, and when the British occupied Istanbul, she escaped to Anatolia. There she set another precedent by enrolling as a private in Atatürk's nationalist army,
earning battlefield promotions to corporal, sergeant, and master sergeant. In the late 1920s, Halide Edib went into exile in
protest against Atatürk's single-party regime—and established
herself as an international literary figure. Her novels, *The Clown
and His Daughter* and *Shirt of Fire*, were translated into the

world's major languages. Equally notable are her memoirs, written in English, which provide a vivid account of contemporary history.

Halide Edib remained a unique figure for her time for transcending the customary sexual and cultural barriers. Meanwhile, the emancipation of women, along with secularism, had become one of the prime aims of Turkey's cultural revolution. With his flair for the dramatic, the childless Kemal Atatürk legally adopted several daughters, one of whom became Turkey's first female pilot and another a leading historian. But for Turkish society as a whole, it should be recalled that the traditional gap between the sexes was never as wide as the aspect of veiled upper-class Ottoman ladies in their secluded harems a century ago—or even the persisting lower class custom of wives walking a pace or two behind their husbands—would suggest.

Back on the farm, there is an established division of labor: while the men take the lead in plowing the fields and tending the animals in the pasture, the women do more than their share of work around the house, in the yard, and in bringing up the girls and younger boys—and in all these spheres they have always been in undisputed charge. For thoroughly practical reasons, these hardworking women never took up the upper-class custom of veiling; instead they wear head scarves. Nor was polygamy ever practiced among the lower social classes: there obviously never were enough women in the population to provide a second wife to more than a privileged caste of pashas, beys, and aghas. In sum, Turkish women in the countryside, even in Atatürk's day, were a good deal closer to being liberated and far more equal to their men than were their idle lady cousins in the palaces or villas of old Istanbul.

The major gap that continued to divide men and women was one of schooling; and for women as for men, education became the chief instrument of change and a clear indicator of progress. In the 1940s, the ratio of boys to girls in the primary grades was about three to one; by the late 1970s, with enrollments six times larger, the ratio had become almost even. Also in the late 1970s, women accounted for one-third of the high school and one-fourth of the university students; and remarkably, the proportion of women among the teachers and professors was equally high.

Women received the right to vote in 1935; and eighteen female deputies took their seats in the one-party Assembly of that year. With the advent of party competition, the number of women deputies declined sharply, reflecting the more traditional orientation of the mass electorate—only to rise again in recent years (to six in 1973 and eleven in 1983). Throughout Turkey, the increasing number of divorces (most of them among childless couples and on grounds of incompatibility) is another indication of social change; significantly, more than half of these now are granted at the wife's request. A recent report noted the increasing number of women in Turkey's managerial ranks: "Modern Turkey is prepared to let women pursue their job ambitions, as long as they follow the ancient sexual rules off the job."[7]

A concrete indication of greater sexual equality among Turkey's lower class is the situation among migrant workers in Germany. The Turkish men typically work in factory or service jobs, and many of them, standing on the assembly line perhaps between fellow workers from Italy and Yugoslavia, have little occasion to learn German. But their wives have opened for themselves a wide market as dressmakers, to the point where tailoring is, next to factory work, the second most frequent occupation of Turks in Germany. (Incidentally, Turkish has no grammatical genders, and the word *terzi* means both "tailor" and "dressmaker.") Close contact with their German clients helps those same Turkish women from small towns or villages become fluent in German and well adapted to German styles of dress and living—a development few observers of the Turkish social scene would have anticipated a decade or two ago.

The temporary restrictions which the military imposed on Turkey's political life after 1980 had the incidental effect of propelling, for the first time in Turkish history, a woman to political prominence. Since Bülent Ecevit was not allowed to join any political parties or make any direct political statements in public or to the press, it was Rahşan Ecevit, his wife and for many years his partner in the full range of his professional activities, who by 1985 emerged as the leader of the Democratic Left Party.[8]

Islam and Secularism from Atatürk to Democracy

One central feature of the Turkish cultural revolution of the 1920s was a turning away from the Islamic traditions of the Ottoman period and the adoption, often by legal fiat, of secular or Western customs. The turban and fez were banned by the so-called Hat Law, and Atatürk himself sported a Panama hat or a visored golf cap instead. The caliphate, by which latter-day sultans had claimed primacy over Muslims of all countries, was abolished. Islamic schools were closed and religious orders outlawed; and the constitutional clause proclaiming Turkey a Muslim state was repealed. The weekly holiday was shifted from Friday to Sunday, and the Islamic lunar calendar, dating from Muhammad's flight from Mecca to Medina in *A.D.* 622, was replaced by the solar Christian (or "international") calendar. The adoption of the Swiss (or "Turkish") Civil Code confirmed the abolition of the Islamic institution of polygamy. The substitution in 1928 of the Latin (or "Turkish") alphabet for the Arabic script in which Turkish had been written for centuries implied another fundamental break with the past.

Some of the practices discarded in the 1920s had been half-hearted compromises of Ottoman times. Thus the brimless fez, attractive because it enabled Muslim men to bow to the ground in prayer, went back to a onetime Venetian fashion of head-dress that became popular in North Africa. In the nineteenth century, the Ottoman government calendar had been shifted to a European solar year, but beginning on March 1 and counted from Muhammad's time in *A.D.* 622; whereas mosques and religious courts retained the traditional Islamic lunar calendar unchanged. The legal system was even more hopelessly fragmented: the muftis' interpretations of Islamic precedent remained paramount in matters of family law and inheritance among Muslims, and a midnineteenth-century codification known as the *Mecelle* attempted to systematize the law of contract and torts among Muslims. Separate priestly or rabbinical courts handled the corresponding matters for Greeks, Armenians, or Jews. European codes were translated for commercial law, and secular courts handled suits where the plaintiff and defendant were of different religions. It was Atatürk's courage in sweeping away this confusion and restoring unity to fundamentals such as legal relations and the reckoning of time that helped rally Turkey's elite behind his program.

The changes in dress and in alphabet were mostly of a symbolic nature, but just for that reason profoundly offensive to conservative sentiment. Thus Atatürk's program might have evoked significant, perhaps fatal, opposition—except that he proclaimed all these reforms in rapid order, between 1924 and 1928, immediately upon consolidating his benevolent one-party dictatorship. When Atatürk's successor, İsmet İnönü, in the 1940s opened the political system to opposition parties and a free press, some of these measures became the objects of delayed controversy. Indeed, there was much apprehension, both in Turkey and abroad, that under democracy, secularism might become the victim of forces of reaction and Islamic revival.

In fact, there was no such violent swing of the pendulum—for a number of distinct and concurrent reasons: the somewhat limited scope of the reforms, the blurring effects of competitive politics itself, and latent divisions within Turkish Islam which democratic processes brought to the fore. Atatürk's secular reforms had not been as sweeping as their ostentatious symbolism might make them appear. For example, the veil was discouraged rather than prohibited; and in any case, the lifting of the veil and the ban on polygamy affected only the affluent segment of the population. Similarly, the change from Arabic to Latin letters was easier to accomplish while only a small literate minority had to relearn their *elif-ba* as ABC.

In certain crucial respects Atatürk continued the Ottoman tradition of blending governmental and religious concerns, thus allowing a measure of synthesis. One striking example is the calendar of public holidays, when offices, banks, schools, and most stores remain closed throughout Turkey. These holidays include January 1 as New Year's Day, May 1 (as the Spring rather than the Labor Holiday), and four anniversaries of Atatürk's own national movement,[9] as well as two major Islamic holidays; and indeed, these two account for as many as seven of the total annual schedule of fourteen-and-a-half free days.

These Islamic holidays, of course, continue to be calculated according to the traditional lunar calendar, and involve no government ceremonies; rather, they mark the highlights of the year as family celebrations, much as do Christmas and Easter in Christian or post-Christian countries. One of these is the Candy Holiday, a three-day celebration of festive meals and visits to friends enjoyed by Turks whether or not they have kept the daytime fast during the preceding holy month of Ramadan. The other is the four-day Sacrifice Feast, commemorating the biblical story of Abraham and Isaac, when sheep marked with colored dye are driven through the streets, then ritually slaughtered, and their cooked meat is shared with family and the poor.

Turkey's flag features the traditional Islamic symbols of a rising crescent and a white star on a red background. Their emotional meaning is powerfully conveyed in a poem written at the height of Turkey's War of Independence (1919–23), whose first two stanzas became the official anthem of the Republic, sung ever since on all festive official occasions. Here, in my own translation close to original rhyme and meter, are those lines:

> Fear not! Red floats the flag from dawn to dawn, nor
>   shall it wane
> While flame yet flickers in my country's last hearth to
>   remain.
> This is my nation's star: forever let it shine!
> This one is mine, my nation's, only mine.
>
> Don't frown, coy crescent, while I go to my ordeal!
> Smile at our race of heroes! Where can you find such
>   strength, such steel?

Or else you cannot answer for the blood spilled in the
fight

For independence, my godly nation's God-entrusted
right.

Atatürk's own principle of *lâiklik* (secularism, laicism) is by
no means the exact equivalent of the separation of church and
state as understood in Europe or the United States. It is far
more stringent in that the Turkish legislature, armed forces,
and universities have no chaplains, and that religious invoca-
tions at public ceremonies would be considered a shocking
lapse liable to legal prosecution. On the other hand, the Islamic
clerical establishment of imams (prayer leaders) and hatibs
(preachers) continues to be appointed, paid, and supervised by
a government agency, which also administers the religious en-
dowments that ensure the upkeep and building of mosques.

The resulting arrangement is not unlike that of the Church of
England or the Lutheran State Church in Sweden. One symbolic difference from Ottoman times is that the highest religious official, who earlier as *şeyhülislâm* had held equal rank
with the grand vezir immediately after the sultan himself, now
is a mere director-general of a department in the prime minister's office; and unlike the Archbishop of Canterbury, he has no
ceremonial function. Like similar institutions in Egypt and
other Sunni-Muslim countries, Turkey's Directorate of Religious Affairs guarantees both funding and government supervision of the clergy—incidentally ensuring that the religious
establishment and its publications will not become vehicles for
fundamentalist or other antigovernment activity.

Since the Ankara government never renounced its involvement in religious affairs, the partisan discussion since the 1940s
has come to focus on the details of relevant government policy.
Early in that debate the political parties vied in proposing minor concessions to Islamic sentiment. Thus İnönü's Republican
People's Party administration opened a theological faculty at
the University of Ankara; expanded the network of schools for
imams and hatibs; allowed the use of scarce foreign exchange
for the pilgrimage to Mecca; and entered the crucial 1950 elec-

tion with a noted Islamic scholar as its prime minister. In 1950, the victorious Democrats, even more dramatically, changed the minaret's prayer call from the "pure Turkish" imposed by Atatürk to its traditional Arabic version.[10] On the other hand, when members of a secret religious order called the Ticanis launched a campaign of smashing public statues (most of them of Atatürk himself) as offending the Islamic ban on graven images, the same Democrat government of Premier Adnan Menderes tightened the laws protecting Atatürk's memory and proceeded to enforce them vigorously.

Taken together, those concessions made by both leading parties have served to depoliticize the religious issue. To be sure, a number of successive Islamic-conservative parties have entered the electoral contests since the 1950s, and occasionally were taken to court for violating the constitutional principle of secularism; but typically these parties, even during the periods of maximum political freedom, garnered no more than five to nine percent of the national vote.[11] By 1974, the major center-left Republican People's Party, upholder of the secularist tradition of Atatürk and İnönü, was able to enter a government coalition with the religiously oriented National Salvation Party. And since the 1970s, successive center-right parties, representing the interests of commercial farming and industry, have been headed by men such as Süleyman Demirel and Turgut Özal, who do not dwell on religious themes in their campaigns but are known to be devout, practicing Muslims in their private lives—much as most American presidents have been believing Christians.

Diversity, Migration, and Tolerance

Competitive politics and the increasing freedom of expression that Turkey has come to enjoy over the years also have brought into the open important divisions within Turkish Islam; and some of these provide a crucial measure of support for secularism itself. The growing pattern of internal and external migration of recent decades has served to blur the urban-rural (and hence the Western-Islamic) contrast; and the democratic process itself has encouraged further pragmatic accommodations.

The largest religious minority in Turkey are the Alevis, who are scattered throughout much of Anatolia. Their version of Islam is related closely to that of the Alawis of Syria and more remotely to Shiite Islam as prevalent in Iran, but clearly distinct from the Sunni, or orthodox, Islam of the majority of Turks. Estimates of their number range from 10 to 20 percent of the total population. [12]

Alevis tend to be staunch supporters of the principle of secularism, in which they see a guarantee of government impartiality between themselves and the Sunni majority; and certain Central Anatolian traditional strongholds of the secularist Republican People's Party in the 1960s and 1970s included Alevi majorities. One of the minor splinter groups called the Unity Party (1966–80, with a maximum of 2.8 percent of the national vote in 1969) directed its appeal more specifically to the Alevis. In 1971, its leaders attracted attention by an unsuccessful suit before the constitutional court alleging that the mere existence, within the government's bureaucracy, of a Directorate of Religious Affairs violated the constitutional principle of secularism.

Another distinctive Islamic group are the brotherhoods (or dervish orders), such as the Bektaşis, Nakşıbendis, and Ticanis. All of these belong to the Sufi, or mystical, branch of Islam, and traditionally have enjoyed a widespread regional and lower-class following. (Thus Atatürk himself, at the beginning of the nationalist war of 1919–23, proved eager to obtain the public endorsement of the head of the Bektaşi order.) Although formally outlawed since 1925, the brotherhoods continue in de facto existence. A rather different direction of Islamic pietism, which lately has developed a strong appeal among some urban intellectuals, is known as Nurculuk ("Followers of Light"). Its founder, Said Nursi, was prosecuted by the authorities of the Republic following the Kurdish uprising of 1925, but in his years of internal exile, he composed a 130-part series entitled *Risale-i Nur* (or "Treatise of Light") interpreting the Koran in modern Turkish and for the contemporary era.

Open organization of Islamic sects or brotherhoods remains prohibited; yet their adherents recognize one another "by certain gestures, the shape of the mustache, the manner of shaking hands, body posture during prayer, or certain turns of phrase." And "in practice these orders are tolerated by the state, as long as they do not meddle in public affairs."[13]

The religious distinctions among Sunnis, Alevis, Bektaşis, and others are just one of the many variations that became apparent as city politicians went out on the rural speaking circuit and villagers migrated to the cities. The population of Anatolian towns and villages includes sizable groups resettled in today's Turkey only in the nineteenth or early twentieth centuries. Among these were Turks from the Balkans (Yugoslavia's Bosnia, Romania's Dobrudja, and various parts of Greece), Albanians, and Turks and other Muslims from Russia (Crimean Tatars, Georgians, and Circassians from the Caucasus). In their new locations in Anatolia, these joined other distinctive ethnic or subethnic groups, such as the Kurds and Arabs of the southeast, the Lazes of the northeast, and nomadic animal herders in the Taurus mountains known as Yörük ("Wanderers") or Turcomans. Each of these groups has its characteristic forms of speech, music, dance, and other customs, but as fellow Muslims, most of them are readily accepted into the Turkish national community. (The only important exception are some of Turkey's Kurdish population; see the following section.)

Clearly, there is as little homogeneity among Turkey's townsmen and villagers as there is among the urban elite—which a generation or two ago was heavily recruited from Balkan towns, including Atatürk's own native city of Salonica, but since then has markedly shifted toward Anatolians including those from the once underdeveloped east. In any case, the meeting between urban and rural Turkey initiated by the democratic reforms of the late 1940s and intensified by the social changes of the 1960s and 1970s has turned out to be no sterile two-way confrontation between Westernization and tradition, but rather a kaleidoscopic, diversified, and dynamic encounter.

Since the late 1960s, the mass migration of Turkish workers to Europe has broken the old middle-class monopoly on direct contact with the West—with social and cultural implications apparent only in future generations.

The competitive desire for economic improvement is the compelling motive that has driven villagers by the hundreds of thousands first to the shantytowns around Turkey's cities and to factory and service jobs in Europe. The influx to the cities is aided by the provision of Middle Eastern customary law that any dwelling that is built on unused land and has four walls and a roof by morning may not be torn down—hence the Turkish name for a shantytown dwelling is *gecekondu*, or "put up overnight." The migration to West Germany and other countries in Western Europe began in the 1960s as Turkey's new status as an associate member of the European Economic Community allowed its citizens to compete in Europe's labor market with its vastly higher wages—so that today as many as 1.8 million Turks reside in West Germany alone.

Back home, this migration, both to the major Turkish cities and to jobs abroad, is sustained by a powerful tradition of social cohesion and mutual support. By the early 1970s, fully one-half of all Turkish villages had seen some of their residents go off to Germany or other European countries, and the common pattern in any given village has been for one or more brothers or cousins to venture forth to the large city in Turkey, or more recently to Germany, leaving one or two others at home to plow and harvest the family's fields. The migrants, in turn, share their larger earnings with the relatives back home, enabling them to do the family farming more efficiently with a tractor rather than with draft animals. Yet such migration was considered temporary: the most cherished ambition of the vast majority of village fathers for their sons was a professional career as a doctor, engineer, teacher, or civil servant—in short, the very jobs available through the expanded system of higher education. And indeed, many of the young men from the villages who go to college in Istanbul or Ankara have been sent there on their families' earnings as migrant workers.

The recent activity of Turkish contractors and export-import traders throughout the Middle East has, conversely, restored the direct contacts between the educated elite and the Muslim Middle East that were rather abruptly cut off in Atatürk's day.

Along the same lines, Ankara's foreign policy has made an important symbolic concession to moderate Sunni-Islamic sentiment by joining the Islamic Conference Organization. And for the 1977 meeting, Turkey even became the ICO's offical host—not in Atatürk's secular capital of Ankara, but in old Istanbul with its sumptuous mosques, sultan's palace, and modern hotels. More recently, President Kenan Evren has combined his personal attendance at an ICO summit with a self-conscious revival of the Atatürk personality cult and vigorous enforcement of the laws protecting the principle of secularism.

One by-product of these recent Turkish diplomatic and commercial contacts with the Middle East has been that wealthy Arabs have begun to buy villas along the Bosporus, with its picturesque, and yet distinctly Islamic, scenery. After the collapse of Beirut as a haven of commerce and tourism Istanbul has been successfully competing with towns such as Amman, Nicosia, and Athens to assume its succession. Thus the borough presidents of some Istanbul suburbs are reported to be studying Arabic; and Arabic inscriptions, outlawed throughout Turkey for over half a century, once again are seen in Istanbul's tourist shops. In sum, Turkey's new function as an economic bridge between Europe and the Middle East helps provide a lucrative resolution for its earlier internal conflict between Westernization and Islamic tradition.

The many separate developments just reviewed add up to a pattern of compromise, tolerance, and pragmatic accommodation between religion and secularism throughout Turkish society. Knowledge of the Arabic script has become virtually extinct except among imams and hatibs. And since literacy in the Latin script has increased so dramatically, religious traditionalists spend far more effort on printing religious tracts in the new alphabet, or recording them on video cassettes, than trying to revive the reading of the Arabic script. One of their recent victories was the appearance on the state television network's religious program of a "TV *hodja*" garbed in the traditional turban.

The vast majority of lower-class Turks, in response to the "Hat Revolution" proclaimed by Atatürk in 1925, chose to adopt the visored cap, enabling them simultaneously to observe the law and to obey the Islamic custom of keeping their head covered, and even (by the simple act of turning the cap back to front) to bow to the ground at prayer time. Nonetheless, the number of Turks who perform the prayer even once a day today declines directly with the size of their community—from 70 percent in the smallest villages to only 24 percent in the major cities. The observance of the Ramadan fast is similarly on the decline, particularly in the cities and among the educated. In Ankara, a surly bank clerk now may feel the need to apologize to his customer saying, "I am a bit edgy today; you see, I am fasting." And while an observant Turk may render thanks to Allah for his success in business by donations to one of the many mosque building societies, attendance at the mosques thus built is lower in Turkey than in any other Muslim country.

Among Turkish Muslims or post-Muslims, just as among Western Christians or post-Christians, those observances that constitute rites of passage—such as circumcision, religious weddings, and Islamic burials—have shown greater resilience than have the more onerous obligations—which for Muslims include five daily prayers and total abstention from food and drink during the daylight hours of the month of Ramadan.[14] Most marriages in the villages and a majority of them in the cities continue to be arranged by the two families, and "bride price" (a monetary or equivalent gift from the groom's to the bride's parents) remains customary in the villages. Yet most urban couples no longer combine the optional religious ceremony with the mandatory one before the public registrar. The *mevlûd* ceremony—a chanted recital of the life, death, and resurrection of Muhammad—remains popular as a requiem on the fortieth day after a relative's death.[15]

All in all, religious observance in Turkey is more widespread than in North America or Northern and Western Europe, though hardly more so than in the Christian countries around the Mediterranean. In today's Turkey, as in the West, religious attitudes range from strict observance to rank indifference. For, between them, the secular laws of the Republic and the steady stream of migration to the cities guarantee that every Turkish adult, man or woman, is now free to decide how religious or irreligious a life he or she wishes to lead.

In addition to the Muslim majority, with its wide range of Sunni orthodoxy, Alevi and Sufi dissent, and agnostic indifference, the population of Turkey includes a small group of non-Muslim minorities. These today constitute a total of fewer than one percent of the population, including Greek Orthodox and Armenian Christians and Jews, and most of them are resident in Istanbul. These religious groups retain the independent communal organizations under their priests or rabbis that characterized the powerful *millet*s of the Ottoman period.[16] Although legally these Christians and Jews enjoy the full rights of Turkish citizenship, and many of the Armenians and Jews speak Turkish as their main language, they neither consider themselves, nor are they generally accepted by others, as Turks. In 1935, Atatürk's one-party regime provided token parliamentary representation for one Greek, one Armenian, and one Jewish deputy from Istanbul; significantly, however, they sat as independents rather than members of the official Republican People's Party, and the practice lapsed after 1946. While these minority groups enjoy some continuing role in the commercial life of Istanbul, their participation in public and political life is negligible.

Expectations and Frustrations

For two or three generations, Turkey has been undergoing a social transformation of unprecedented sweep. The Islamic and multinational empire of the sultans was reborn as a secular nation-state; traditional law, education, and writing yielded to their European equivalents. An illiterate peasantry has gone to school and moved into town. The gasoline engine and the television set have overcome rural isolation, and an agrarian economy has industrialized. A once traditional and patriarchal society is moving rapidly toward egalitarian and democratic values.

These multiple and concurrent trends, as we saw, have acquired an irresistible momentum. Spokesmen for Islamic tradition claim that Islam is the most modern and technologically advanced of religions. Instead of demands for a reversal of the nationalist and democratizing reforms of the last six decades, the major trend is toward a constructive and tolerant blending of traditional and modern life. Nonetheless, a cultural and social upheaval such as Turkey has undergone is not without its human and social costs.

The urban population has quadrupled since 1950—which is to say that a majority of city dwellers are recent migrants from the country. Yet the better employment that lured them from their villages does not materialize for all. The further migration to Germany brings the Turkish worker into direct contact with the marvels of an advanced industrial society—and massive ethnic prejudice and discrimination. Back home in Turkey, television programs such as "Dallas" and "The Duchess of Duke Street" became widely popular in the 1970s—and keenly reminded Turkish viewers how much their own urban or shantytown surroundings contrasted with the glamorized vision of American and British material life projected on the screen.

A particular group of Turkish citizens that has reason for feeling left out in the ongoing social transformation is the Kurdish-speaking minority of the southeast. By and large, the ethnic or subethnic differences among Turkey's Muslim population have begun to disappear—as the late Ottoman Empire attracted refugees from Russia or the Balkans such as Tatars, Circassians, and Bosniaks; and as internal migration and economic development gave them the opportunity to blend into the general Turkish population. There also is an Arab minority, about one percent of the total population, but it is concentrated along the Syrian border, where they constitute about one-third of the Hatay province—and have always had the choice of assimilation or emigration to neighboring Arab countries. By contrast, the Kurdish population (according to the most recent census figures of 1965) constitutes eight percent of Turkey's total; is the resident majority in eight southeastern provinces bordering on Iran and Iraq; and has no national state of its own.[17]

In 1925, these Kurdish districts were among the centers of an Islamic-conservative rebellion against the newly constituted

Republic of Turkey, and much of the region has been under martial law ever since. Official policy since that time does not permit the use of Kurdish in schools or in the press, and indeed the censuses since 1970 have not even included the earlier questions about mother tongue. Meanwhile the age-old pattern of clan warfare among Kurds in the southeastern mountains persists, and the official anti-Kurdish policy has enabled a small minority, with Soviet arms smuggled from Iraq and more recently Syria, to carry on sporadic terrorist acts in the name of national liberation.

For the urban migrants, the hardships have been greatest in times of economic crisis, as recession brought massive unemployment, inflation steeply raised living costs, or foreign exchange crises resulted in acute shortages. Although times of prosperity eased the unemployment, they made all the more glaring the economic gap between the working poor or unemployed and the prosperous middle class. Education, we noted, serves as a major avenue of social ascent; yet the mass influx to the universities of Istanbul and Ankara in the 1970s created overcrowded lecture halls with hundreds, and indeed thousands, of students, and a hard-to-bridge gap between students and faculty.

It was in the urban slums and universities of the 1970s that the multiple frustrations of economic gaps and social displacement translated themselves into gang warfare between groups mouthing leftist or rightist slogans and into sporadic terrorism against the population at large.

As social friction and frustration were mounting, it happened that the economy was going through its dreary decennial cycle of prosperity, crisis, and collapse; and the political system into a state of paralysis. After the elections of the 1970s, the Islamic and ultranationalist parties often commanded the few crucial votes that might make or break a coalition government, thereby increasing their leeway for acting at the margin of the law. Terrorists of the left and militant Kurdish groups could count on training in the PLO's Lebanese camps and a steady supply of Soviet weapons from Syria or Bulgaria, or across the Black Sea; and terrorists of the right benefited from the military connections of their leaders—or indeed, at one point, their control of the Ministry of Customs.

The military regime of 1980–83, through its wholesale roundup of arms and arrest of violent dissidents, put a sudden stop to this indiscriminate violence both in Turkish cities and (with few exceptions) in the Kurdish border regions. Above all, Turkey's rapid economic development in the mid-1980s provided new opportunities for positive integration of those whom society had left orphaned in the past. In view of Turkey's religious homogeneity, and in light of earlier experience in the economically advanced parts of Turkey, one may assume, for example, that the new agricultural and industrial opportunities opened up in southeastern Turkey by the giant hydroelectric Keban and Atatürk dams (the latter scheduled for completion in 1988) will do a good deal to integrate Turkey's Kurdish minority economically and socially—more, at any rate, than the previous half-century of economic neglect and pretending that Kurds do not exist.

Once again, new spurts of economic and social development are sure to arouse new expectations—and frustrations. But Turkey has overcome its interval of political deadlock and terrorism and (as we shall see in Chapter 4) is developing a stable two-party system. Hence one may expect that future social dislocations will enliven the political debate, force government and opposition to vie for practical solutions acceptable to a wide variety of groups of voters—and in sum, launch a constructive political process that, far from destroying democracy, will strengthen it.

Three

Turkey's Economy: Widening Frontiers

Diverse Resources and Hard Work

In contrast to most Middle Eastern countries, with their fertile valleys separated by vast deserts, Turkey's geography is distinctly Mediterranean. Steep mountains alternate with stretches of dry plateau, fertile plains, and lush coastlines. That same variety is reflected in Turkey's abundant agricultural and mineral resources and its diverse population.

The sunny hills and broad valleys of Turkey's western region along the Aegean Sea, and the wide Thracian plain to the north of the Marmara Sea, bear fruits, vegetables, and domestic livestock in great abundance. Traditionally, raisins, figs, hazelnuts, and tobacco have been among Turkey's most reliable and lucrative exports shipped from Izmir, Istanbul, and lesser ports; and melons and tree fruit abound for local consumption. In Turkey's south-central region, around Adana, the rivers cascading off the Taurus mountains toward the Mediterranean used to form a marshy coastal plain; but once those swamps were drained through efforts of nineteenth-century sultans and settled with Turkish immigrants from the Balkans and the Caucasus, they became a rich center for cotton cultivation, thus adding to the list of export staples. By contrast, the northeastern coast along the Black Sea is dominated by steep mountainsides, and the resulting moist, subtropical climate proves ideal for the cultivation of rice and several varieties of tea.

The central plateau that stretches between those coastal mountains is rather dry, as is the large southeastern plain along the Syrian frontier. Many parts of those regions are ideal for grazing and thus serve as the centers for the raising of live-stock—sheep, cattle, and horses. Donkeys serve for transport for those who cannot afford a horse; and buffalo are still widely used as work animals on the smaller farms. Goats are appreci-ated for their milk and cheese; and of course the long-haired variety, with its soft, resilient wool, is known the world over as the "Angora" goat—Angora being an older name for Turkey's capital of Ankara. Only domestic pigs are absent, since Turks, as Muslims, are not allowed to eat pork; and, not surprisingly, the Turkish word for pig, or wild boar, is a byword not for uncleanliness or gluttony but for cruelty.

At the very center of the Anatolian plateau, there is a small stretch of desert around the Tuz Gölü (Salt Lake); but most other portions of Turkey's central and southeastern plains are traversed by major rivers. The Sakarya and Kızıl Irmak ("Red River") flow in wide loops through the central plateau toward the Black Sea, and the Murad and Karasu ("Black Water") cut through the eastern mountains, joining to form the Euphrates. Farther east there is the Tigris, which, like the Euphrates, crosses the frontier southward—eventually forming that re-gion which the ancient Greeks dubbed "Mesopotamia" (or "The Land Between the Rivers") and the Arabs "al-Iraq." These headwaters of the Euphrates provide the sites for the giant hydroelectric Keban Dam, which Turgut Özal helped build as a young engineer, and the even larger Atatürk irriga-tion dam now under construction. In the central and southeast-ern highlands, there are many lesser rivers whose dams and canals, built in the 1950s and 1960s, converted much pasture to the planting of cereals, including wheat, barley, and corn.

The mountains along Turkey's Black Sea coast in the north rise to a height of 9,000 feet, and the Taurus chain along the Mediter-ranean in the south, to over 11,000 feet. In the eastern half of the country, those two chains intertwine and rise to over 16,000 feet, the highest peak being the 16,946-foot Mount Ararat, the leg-endary landing place for Noah's Ark after the Great Flood, and today the border between Turkey and Soviet Armenia. Those mountain regions not only contribute a substantial share of Turkey's (and most of Syria's and Iraq's) water resources, but also are rich in minerals. Among these, chromium and manganese became major export items in the 1930s; whereas iron ore mined in the east supplies the domestic steel industry. The country's major coal mining center, near Zonguldak on the Black Sea, produces mostly lignite (or "brown coal"), which, in comparison to anthracite (or "hard coal"), is low in caloric value and high in sulfur content.

Unfortunately for Turkey, only a few traces of petroleum have been found under its soil—the oil-rich Mosul region, which remained in dispute after the 1923 peace treaty, having been subsequently awarded to Iraq. Exploration for offshore oil under the Aegean Sea was begun in the 1970s, but soon halted as a result of a complex Greek-Turkish border dispute (see Chapter 5). As a result, Turkey since the 1970s has done its best to reduce petroleum imports by cutting hidden subsidies for gasoline and heating oil and by shifting electricity generation to thermal (lignite-burning) power plants and hydroelectricity. In the longer run, electricity from water power and nuclear energy, rather than lignite, also promises to help lift the thick cloud of pollution which hangs heavily over the broad valley of the capital of Ankara and occasionally even over the wind-swept hills of Istanbul.

Disregarding the shortage of domestic oil, the richness of Turkey's natural endowment is best appreciated in comparison with other nations. The typical country of Asia and Africa contributes to the world economy a single mineral or agricultural product—Saudi Arabia petroleum, Morocco phosphates, Ghana cocoa, Liberia iron ore, Zambia copper, Sri Lanka tea, Malaysia tin; and naturally such "one-crop economies" are highly vulnerable to sudden price swings in the market for that single commodity. Other countries must rely heavily on imported raw materials (Japan, South Korea), or earn their keep by processing imported goods for reexport (Taiwan, Hong Kong, Singapore).

Turkey, happily, has a multicrop economy. Exports include tobacco, cotton, hazelnuts, livestock, raisins, and cereals, in that approximate order of total value; a growing share of manufactured goods, such as cotton yarns and textiles, cement, glass, and even assembled motor vehicles; and a smaller but solid amount of mineral ores, such as manganese, borates, and chromium.[1]

It is a rare drought that affects tobacco, cotton, wheat, and raisins all at once; and cotton thread and metal ores are subject to different cycles of foreign demand. Above all, Turkey, in contrast to the prevailing Asian and African one-crop (or single-ore) pattern, is relatively self-sufficient: the total value of exports and imports was under 13 percent of the gross domestic product in the 1960s, under 18 percent in the 1970s, rising above one-quarter only in 1982.

In addition to these exports of Turkish agricultural, industrial, and mineral goods, a dramatic development for Turkey's economy has been its intensive new connections with Western Europe and the Middle East—whose substantial contribution to Turkey's economy and balance of payments has already been noted: Turkish workers in West Germany in the 1960s and early 1970s, and more recently, construction firms in Saudi Arabia and Libya. In the 1980s, Iraq and Iran, after cutting off much of each other's trade across the Gulf, found that the most convenient trade connection with Europe for both of them went across neutral Turkey.

As an early result of Özal's liberalization measures, the level of remittances from Turkish workers and firms abroad has risen above $2 billion every year since 1980.

This not only illustrates Turkey's geographic function as a bridge between Western Europe and the Middle East; but also testifies to the versatility and enterprise of Turks of all social strata.

The Tradition of Government Enterprise and Regulation

The Özal government's decision to sell bonds for the Bosporus Bridge to private investors marked a radical departure from a long tradition of economic policy. From the founding of the Turkish Republic in the 1920s, the state had been the chief architect and promoter of the country's economic develop-

ment. Government agencies had run the railways that linked
Istanbul with the Anatolian hinterland, and the shipping lines
along Turkey's Mediterranean and Black Sea coasts. Banks or
corporations owned by the government had developed the
mining resources of the mountainous east and contracted with
foreign companies to construct the country's first steel mill.
And the government had been involved, on and off, in super-
vising the marketing of Turkey's agricultural produce overseas.

By the 1930s, government enterprise, or *étatisme* (the Turkish
word is borrowed from the French), had been laid down as a
fundamental principle in the program of Kemal Atatürk's government party and enshrined in the constitution of the Republic. By the 1940s, the government through its ministries,
independent agencies, and subsidiaries of its wholly owned
banks had become the nation's major industrial producer, largest employer, and leading exporter. Yet it is important to note
that this Turkish system of government enterprise was supported by middle-class rather than working-class interests; and
that the ideological impetus behind it had been not socialist but
nationalistic.

In the days of the Ottoman sultans, concessions for banking,
shipping, and mining had been granted to European entrepreneurs. Under the so-called capitulations, such foreign companies were exempt from Ottoman laws and taxation—and even
members of the religious minorities of Istanbul (Greeks, Jews,
Armenians) had found it advantageous to register their companies in the name of foreign nationals so as to reap those same
benefits. Unable to pay its debts to foreign banks, the Ottoman
government by 1881 had been forced to turn over the very
collection of its revenues to foreigners; and naturally, this entire system of foreign privileges and controls was deeply re-
sented by the civil servants who formed the core of the aspiring
Muslim-Turkish middle class.

When, following the War of Independence, the Turkish Republic in 1923 was recognized by the European powers as a
nation among sovereign equals, its founders considered the final
settlement of that Ottoman debt and the abolition of the centu-

ries-old capitulations to be their greatest economic achievements. It was in that process that the country's railways, steamships, and telephones (as well as the trolley cars and gas and electricity lines of Istanbul) were transferred from foreign ownership to national or municipal management. Also, the population exchange provisions of the 1923 peace treaty with Greece involved the Ankara government in a major program of land distribution and resettlement. In other words, Turkish state enterprise resulted not from the wholesale expropriation of any domestic class of private entrepreneurs, but rather from the assertion of political independence—the victory of a new nation over the economic and political forces of colonialism.

Nor was Turkey's new pattern of government enterprise out of line with prevailing international trends. Throughout Europe, railroads, telephones, electricity, and urban transport were traditionally run as public services by national or local authority. The Great Depression of the 1930s prompted Western governments to even more extensive economic intervention, such as tariff protection, support of agricultural prices, and public works to combat unemployment—from Hitler's "Reichsarbeitsdienst" to Roosevelt's "New Deal."

Although President İnönü's government kept Turkey out of World War II, six years of military mobilization and the disruption of normal trade patterns involved the government in economic activity on an unprecedented scale. While one group of officials drew up lengthening lists of price regulations and currency controls, others launched a propaganda campaign to promote "local goods" over scarce imports, and still others imposed a set of arbitrary measures of taxation ostensibly directed against wartime profiteers.

With the turn toward democracy in the late 1940s, the policy of *étatisme* thus became a logical target for attack by the newly formed Democrat Party (DP). Among the party's founders, Celâl Bayar had been the first director of the İş Bank, which under his aegis developed into Turkey's major private banking concern. Bayar had also served in the government during brief spells of economic liberalization in the 1920s and 1930s, and had been İnönü's rival for Atatürk's succession. Another founder of the DP, Adnan Menderes, was a commercial farmer from the Aegean coast and opposed to İnönü's recently announced program of land redistribution. Naturally enough, the Democrats under Bayar and Menderes were enthusiastically backed by private business interests in Istanbul and Izmir and by landowners throughout the country.

When the Democrats assumed office in 1950, they removed most of the foreign trade restrictions of the previous decades; yet there was no wholesale dismantling of the government's economic activity. For one thing, the incoming party was waiting to replace the officeholders of the past with its own personnel, and the state economic agencies loomed large among the available prizes. For another, the Democrats' overwhelmingly rural supporters proved eager to shift the existing government machinery from industrial toward agricultural development. Instead of railroads and steel mills, the DP government thus gave priority to building a road network by which farm produce could reach urban or overseas markets, and to new dams and irrigation canals that could convert additional land to farming. The Ankara government began to supply farm credit on a large scale, and U.S. foreign aid facilitated the import of farm machinery.

The result was a broad shift from the age-old pattern of subsistence farming toward commercial agriculture and an increase in farm productivity that has continued to the present. In 1953 there were only some 3,000 tractors in use on all Turkish farms; by 1981 their number had risen to half a million. Since the early 1950s, the annual consumption of fertilizer has risen a thousandfold, resulting in a doubling of the annual wheat harvest and a tripling of the yield of Turkey's rice paddies. And in the 1950s, Turkey briefly became one of the world's leading exporters of wheat.

Rural development and the energies released by the transition to democracy thus produced an impressive economic upsurge. Yet the country's changing economic fortunes and shifting political regimes from the 1950s to the 1970s had the net effect of further expanding the government's economic role. During a brief period of military intervention (1960–61), a State

Planning Organization was set up to coordinate the government's economic efforts, and from 1963 to 1978, this agency drew up successive Five-Year Plans—mostly along the lines of "indicative planning" used in France's mixed economy. The entrenched multiparty system of Turkey's Second Republic encouraged the parties to identify more clearly with economic interests: the Justice Party with business interests in Istanbul, Izmir, and other cities; the Republican People's Party with organized labor, government officialdom, and urban intellectuals; the National Salvation Party with trading firms in the provincial towns; and the left-wing Turkish Labor Party with the more militant labor unions.

This interest group struggle among and outside the parties was accentuated during the long periods when, in the absence of any legislative majority, governments depended on uneasy coalitions or served in a caretaker capacity. Aspiring social groups came to look to their Ankara representatives to meet their urgent demands: social security for employees, minimum wages for industrial workers, the right to strike for their unions, easy credit for farmers and support prices for their products, low-cost housing for middle-income city dwellers, price controls for consumers' essentials, and so forth. Chambers of commerce and industry, moderate and militant labor unions, and a variety of professional associations intensified those group pressures.[2] And in the shifting parliamentary alignments of the 1970s, key supporters of the government of the day came to insist on more direct and tangible benefits: public works expenditures in their local districts, import restrictions on foreign competitors, and more generous government contracts for their particular lines of business.

Tariffs and Subsidies: The Urge to Turn Inward

Turkey's expanding system of state enterprise and government economic regulation thus developed in response to the growing demands of domestic groups roused to consciousness first by the national revolution of the 1920s, and later, and with greater intensity, by the democratic revolution of the 1950s and the multiparty politics of the 1960s. Its drawbacks became increasingly apparent in Turkey's foreign economic relations in the 1960s and 1970s.

In the political and cultural spheres, the problem of keeping Turkey in tune with world trends had been brilliantly resolved by Atatürk's revolution of the 1920s and 1930s. The Turkish people had rejected their Ottoman imperial past and all Western colonialist designs upon them, reorganized themselves into a nation, and been accepted into the European family of nations. The new Turkish Republic thus had inaugurated an unprecedented period of peace, and even of friendship and alliance, with former antagonists in the West. Early in this new era and under Atatürk's personal aegis, Turkey's elite had resolved its former doubts in embracing Western standards of art, science, and the privacy of religion. A vastly expanded system of education soon made those new values available to all Turks—and in due course, began to produce Turkish scientists and artists of international standing.

In economics, alas, the same logic of political initiative and governmental fiat, intended to bring Turkey up to international standards, miscarried. The founders of the Republic were on solid ground in embracing industrialization as a major goal for the new nation. Similarly, the initial task of expanding the country's infrastructure of railroads, ports, and telegraph lines was one that men of military background, such as the ministers of public works of the young Republic, found entirely congenial. But the danger was that national economic planning by former military officers would soon result in a self-fulfilling prophecy: a domestic economy ideally suited as a source of emergency procurement in times of siege.[3]

In Turkey's foreign trade, the peace treaty of 1923, while abolishing the capitulations and other foreign privileges, had imposed a moratorium on tariff duties; and Turkish leaders took it for granted that, once full jurisdiction over customs was attained by 1929, tariffs would be imposed so as to protect indigenous infant industries from foreign competition. During the previous half-century (indeed for as long as statistics had been kept), the Ottoman Empire and the early Republic had run adverse balances of trade year after year. Now, upon attaining tariff sovereignty, Turkey from 1930 to 1937 achieved its first positive trade balances—by the drastic expedient of throttling imports back to half or less of their previous levels.

During the years of World War II, with Turkey a neutral enclave among the Middle Eastern, Balkan, and Russian theaters of war, foreign trade dwindled to a minimum, and government price controls tended to accentuate some of the resulting shortages. At war's end, Turkish economic planners, instead of opening the economy to new opportunities of foreign trade, resumed their previous strategy of industrialization by import substitution. The aim was to keep Turkey's trade in balance not by stimulating exports but by encouraging local firms to produce what merchants had previously imported; and the chief methods of encouragement were tariffs, quotas, or currency restrictions on foreign imports. The difficulty, of course, was that the privileged industries thus created were likely to be run by inexperienced managers and to be committed to technologies soon outdated—yet shielded from any pressure for change. Pampered by protective tariffs, few "infant" industries would find the strength, or indeed the will, to "grow up." By the 1980s, in the judgment of one knowledgeable observer, it was only some of the oldest of Turkey's industries dating to the 1930s, such as cement, glass, leather, and textiles, that were ready to hold their own against international competition.[4]

The government's goal to safeguard the value of Turkey's currency proved just as elusive. The tighter the restrictions imposed on foreign transactions, the greater became the potential profit in circumventing them—and the greater the determination of government officials to impose additional regulations. Once again it became clear that the only logical outcome of the inward-oriented policy of import substitution would be autarky—the complete suspension of foreign trade.

Meanwhile, the advent of democratic politics with its growing pressures on the government budget created an inflationary spiral that reduced the value of the Turkish lira abroad —except that government controls over foreign currency transactions maintained the fiction of its earlier, higher values. Thus, between 1946 and 1958, the Turkish lira on foreign markets had fallen by more than two-thirds, from 35 to 11 U.S. cents, while Turkey's Central Bank maintained the original rate. This blatant overvaluation was in direct contradiction to the government's goal of import substitution—for an overvalued currency stimulates imports and inhibits exports, thus inviting ever larger trade deficits. Since the regulatory climate defeated any government efforts at attracting foreign investment, those mounting deficits would increasingly have to be covered by foreign aid and, failing that, foreign loans from governments or private banks. And this mounting appetite for credits, of course, aggravated the ultimate risk of collapse, as in Turkey's periodic insolvencies and forced devaluations in 1958, 1970, and 1978–80.

The crisis of the late 1970s far exceeded the dimensions of the earlier ones. Following the 1970 devaluation, Turkey had briefly achieved an impressive economic growth rate, and from 1971 through 1973, its foreign trade and currency transactions showed a healthy current account surplus. Then, in 1974, came OPEC's oil price revolution which all at once doubled the import bill; and a dispute over Cyprus (see Chapter 5), which severely reduced American aid for the remainder of the decade. On Turkey's political arena, the 1973 and 1977 elections produced a deadlock among the parties and an alternation of weak coalitions and caretaker cabinets. A wave of labor unrest created unprecedented disruptions in the economy[5]; and the government took to overspending and deficit financing on an unprecedented scale. Soon, annual inflation rates rose steeply, from 17 percent in 1976 to 110 percent in 1980. By 1977 Turkey was reduced once again to borrowing from foreign private banks at sharply rising interest rates; and by 1978 its Central Bank was unable to keep its repayments on schedule—the total outstanding international debt having reached $13.8 billion. After nearly two years of protracted negotiation, an austerity program was adopted in January 1980, including a devaluation of the Turkish lira from TL 47 to TL 70 to the dollar (or 2.13 to 1.43 U.S. cents per Turkish lira).

Decades of inward-oriented policies of import substitution and currency control had failed to bring Turkey up to international standards or to self-sufficiency. Instead, they had caught the country's economy in an ever-sharper contradiction between demand and supply. The better-off Turkish citizens, educated in the Western fashion and eager to travel abroad, quickly developed a taste for refrigerators, washing machines, ready-made quality clothes, automobiles, television sets, and cassette recorders. Turkish consumers had no trouble in adapting their demand to the latest offerings of the international market. In sharp contrast, those citizens, who, as industrial producers, were responsible for supplying such fashionable wares were kept in splendid isolation from the corresponding international methods of production. To maintain that ever-wider disparity required import and currency regulations of growing complexity. The mounting costs of the operation were borne, in part, by a third group of Turkish citizens, who, by a notable gap in the isolationist system, were allowed to go to Europe to participate in the international market as common laborers; and in part by foreign aid and bank loans at usurious rates—until devaluations and debt reschedulings short-circuited the growing tension.

In sum, in matters of politics and education, in science, art, and literature, Turkey since the days of Atatürk had taken its standards from abroad and been proud to achieve them at home; but in economics that same pride had come before a fall. Consumers were only too eager to make the leap to prevailing international standards—while shortsighted government policies confirmed the producers' reluctance to do likewise. Having shielded the individual producer from the inconvenient daily discipline of foreign competition, those inward-oriented government policies forced the whole nation headlong into the far more painful collective discipline of decennial devaluations and austerity programs as imposed by foreign lenders. By contrast, Turkey's liberalization policies since 1980 have increased the daily risks to individuals, but are designed to minimize the major long-run hazards to the national economy as a whole.

State Planning versus Individual Initiative: A Liberal Revolution?

Taking the early development of the Turkish Republic together with the later crises, government involvement in the economy can claim some solid achievements. Crucial industrial sectors, such as mining and steelmaking, have built a firm foundation for further industrial growth. The expanding transportation network by rail, highway, coastal shipping, and more recently, civil aviation has put the major cities and towns throughout the country within easy reach and thus helped transform all of Turkey into a single commercial market. Between 1950 and 1980, the network of surfaced roads throughout the country quadrupled, and the fleet of cars, trucks, and buses multiplied more than thirtyfold. Easier access to remote regions caused a dramatic improvement in health and education. Improved health, in turn, has meant a higher net birth rate, while increased geographic mobility has encouraged the growing rural population to migrate in search of new economic opportunity to the sprawling towns and cities.

Television, first introduced in the late 1960s, has spread rapidly to all cities and towns, as well as the growing number of villages served by the national electricity grid. The transmission stations, although operated by the government, carry advertising, so that the TV screen notably contributes to the stimulation and standardization of consumer tastes in Turkey's rapidly expanding market.

Along with such unquestioned economic benefits, the drawbacks of government management of the economy have become increasingly apparent. Protectionism provided hidden subsidies and created pressure groups insistent on maintaining or increasing them. Wage controls and union organization inhibited labor mobility and productivity in some of the most advanced economic sectors. Price controls for essentials encouraged consumption, thus requiring even more expensive subsidies.

Turkey is still completing the secular process of transforming itself from subsistence agriculture into an industrial economy. It was not until 1974 that the contribution of industry to the gross national product began to exceed that of agriculture— which continues to employ a majority of the working population. Only in 1981 did the value of industrial exports begin to exceed that of agricultural ones. In this steady process of industrialization, public enterprise had at first been essential in creating much of the necessary infrastructure; yet at a later stage of that same process, government regulation, by its very nature, came to weigh most heavily upon those industrial and commercial sectors that should have provided the engine for the country's further transformation.

Meanwhile, within Turkey's traditional pattern of mixed public-private economy, the country by the 1960s and 1970s was developing what had been so clearly lacking in the 1920s— a distinctive and growing class of commercial farmers, large traders, and industrial entrepreneurs. Ordinary Turks had long inclined toward a cynical view of some of the government's economic efforts. "Must have been local goods!" became a standard exclamation when household gadgets malfunctioned in the 1940s. And a newspaper cartoon in the 1950s depicted two workmen on shore eyeing the arrival of a ship laden with camera-spangled foreigners. "For years we have made publicity to attract tourism," says one to the other, "and here are the tourists: now let's start building hotels *immediately*." But by the 1970s the spokesmen for Turkey's new entrepreneurial class stood ready to dispute with the more established class of government officials not just the details of government management but the very principles of economic policy. And a number of nationwide business organizations began to compile a stream of economic data, analyses, and forecasts that could rival in comprehensiveness and accuracy those provided by the government's Central Bank, State Planning Organization, and other offices.

In the growing debate between spokesmen for the government and the private sector, periodic crises served to strengthen the critics' case: spiraling budget deficits, galloping inflation, social unrest at times of economic downturns, mounting foreign debts, and the country's recurrent need to reschedule payments on its foreign loans. It was Turgut Özal's promise of a consistent, far-ranging economic program to avoid such periodic debacles that won him the support first of the Demirel government and Turkey's creditors in 1979, then of Evren and his fellow generals in 1980, and in 1983 of a majority of Turkish voters.

The short-term successes of Özal's economic program were remarkable. The foreign debt was rescheduled in the early 1980s, and by 1986 Turkey had registered the highest growth rates within the OECD. By this time, moreover, the foreign debt of $14 billion that precipitated Turkey's payments crisis of 1978 came to seem paltry compared to the hundreds of billions run up by Latin American debtor countries. Meanwhile, with the advice of leading experts from the U.S. private sector, Özal's government launched its program of "privatization" of state economic enterprises, for which the sale of the Bosporus Bridge provided the dramatic opening.

Turkey, its frontiers now open to foreign capital, is becoming an attractive setting for foreign investment. With a population of over 50 million people, it offers the largest domestic market between Italy and India, and its lively trade with Middle Eastern neighbors means that a wider regional market also is accessible to international firms that may decide to locate in Istanbul, Izmir, or other centers. Turkey in the early 1980s became particularly attractive for American and European investments in agribusiness, processed foods, textiles, and to some extent electronics manufacturing and regional banking. In terms of openness to foreign investment, its nearest competitors to the east were in Singapore and Hong Kong. Turkey's wage level is still about one-fourth that of Western Europe, but the massive migration of her workers to temporary jobs in Germany is vastly adding to the pool of industrial skills.

Turkish businessmen have begun to prove themselves in competition for Middle Eastern construction contracts—while the Özal government's devolution of former state monopolies is opening for them new opportunities at home. And with the dismantling of protective tariffs, they have a strong incentive for meeting the challenge of foreign competition in Turkey's own industrial market.

It may well take until the turn of the century before Turkey can rival the earlier economic accomplishments of the so-called NICs, or newly industrializing countries, such as Taiwan and South Korea. Yet over that longer term, and if the new outward orientation endures, Turkey's unique access to a large domestic and larger regional market may well enable it to secure a leading place among those NICs.

The road to such achievement, nonetheless, will be far from smooth. How well Turkey will be able to stay the new course will depend both on foreign economic constellations and, above all, on the domestic political response. A country such as Turkey is sure to face opposite pressures in attempting to close the wide gap that decades of inward orientation have opened up between domestic and foreign economic realities.

There is a similar difficulty in balancing short-term losses against long-term gains. The pains of any basic readjustment such as Turkey undertook after 1980 are felt automatically and almost at once; whereas the benefits, such as an influx of foreign investments at home and the new opportunities for Turkish business abroad, can only develop more slowly.

Thus by the mid-1980s, Özal's critics among foreign and domestic businessmen began to complain that the cuts in government subsidies and the devolution of deficit-ridden state enterprises—aside from the ostentatious sales of bonds for bridges and hydroelectric dams—had barely started, and that government deficits too often were covered by expanding the money supply. Among the general population, unemployment, inflation, and the high cost of living remained the major complaints; for, by 1985 Turkey's return to democracy had proceeded far enough for the domestic critics in the press and the opposition parties to have found their voice. Annual inflation, which Özal had promised to bring down to 25 percent, remained closer to 50 percent. For Turkey's producers and consumers alike, the cost of credit rose sharply. The dismantling of tariffs and quotas made foreign goods available—whereas devaluation substantially raised their prices. Generally, the phasing out of price controls and subsidies added to the pressures on the household budget.

Some of this economic dissatisfaction was becoming evident in the parliamentary by-election of September 1986, as Özal's Motherland Party saw its vote in a sampling of local districts decline sharply to 32.1 percent and Demirel's True Path Party move to second place with 23.6 percent. By the time of the next regularly scheduled national vote in 1988, there is little question that Özal will be facing an even stronger challenge from Demirel, but also a strong and united opposition on the left that will appeal to factory workers, small farmers, and the unemployed. Nonetheless, the leading leftist groups, consolidated by 1985 in the Social Democratic-Populist Party, proclaimed their dedication not just to social justice and redistribution but also to efficiency in a mixed private-public economy. The appeal of Demirel and Özal's other rivals on the right will have to be that they will carry out the original liberal economic program even better than did Özal himself.

In sum, whatever the specific election results of 1988 and beyond, Turkish economic policies in the foreseeable future are likely to alternate, as do those of Western European countries, between business-oriented liberalism and a moderate form of democratic socialism, with phases of the business cycle and personalities of political leaders setting the pace of the alternation.

The longer-range economic prospects would seem only to be strengthened by this emerging political constellation. Özal's reform program in its initial phase obtained stronger political support than any other program since the 1950s. His popularity began to decline at midterm—yet in the long run, it is clear that democracy offers some of the same advantages as does an outward-oriented economy. By subjecting the government to the daily discipline of criticism, and to the occasional alternation of elected majorities, it avoids the prolonged, artificial calm and the ultimate sudden shifts and violent explosions characteristic of authoritarian regimes.

Four

The Hard Road to Democracy

The 1980 Coup and Its Aftermath

In the major cities of Turkey in the small hours of September 12, 1980, tanks rumbled through the streets; military police arrested one hundred leading politicians; and on the government radio, Chief of Staff General Kenan Evren announced the seizure of executive and legislative power by the country's armed forces. Broad segments of Turkish opinion were inclined to take the generals at their word that this was a coup to restore democracy, not to destroy it. Unlike the classic colonels' coup, which splits the army, sharpens ideological divisions, and succeeds by plot and violence, this was a generals' coup effected without bloodshed by the armed forces as a whole.

The tanks soon withdrew from the streets. Patrolling soldiers ordered residents to paint over the inflammatory political graffiti of left- and right-wing extremists on the walls in their neighborhood. In the months before the coup, political violence throughout the country had cost twenty to thirty lives a day. Now a young mother in an Ankara slum remembered the eve of the coup as the first night when there was no shooting in the streets.[1] The ousted prime minister, Süleyman Demirel, and opposition leader, Bülent Ecevit, found themselves confined with their wives at a seaside motel. Turgut Özal, chief economic planner of the deposed civilian government, was given even broader powers in conducting the delicate negotiations with Turkey's foreign creditors. The generals and admirals of the National Security Council, newly installed as the country's rulers, skipped a major military ceremony to attend briefings from ranking civil servants on the problems of each major government department.

This was the third military intervention in Turkey's politics since the country had begun its move toward democracy in the late 1940s, and this time the interval of military rule was to last longer than previously. It took two years until a new constitution was drafted and submitted to the voters, and another year before national elections, at the end of 1983, established a civilian parliament and cabinet.

Even then, important restrictions remained. The referendum that approved the 1982 constitution also elected General Evren to a seven-year presidency—unopposed. Both the constitution and Evren's personal style made it clear that, at least in matters of foreign policy and internal security, he would be more than a ceremonial head of state. Martial law and press censorship remained in effect, to be lifted only gradually, province by province, in the years to come. The Turkish universities, which in the 1970s had become hotbeds of left- and right-wing violence, were summarily reorganized by a commission handpicked by the outgoing military rulers, with some ideological supervision of the curriculum, punitive transfers for faculty members, and petty restrictions on personal appearance: no headscarves for female students, no chinbeards for male faculty.

In the shift from military to civilian rule, all the political parties of the pre-1980 period were outlawed, their parliamentarians banned from political activity for five years and their top leaders for as long as a decade;[2] and even newly founded parties and their leaders required official approval to enter the electoral contest.

All these restrictions were intended to leave the field in the 1983 election campaign to two parties founded with the junta's express encouragement—the Nationalist Democracy Party of retired General Turgut Sunalp, envisaged as the future government party, and the Populist Party headed by Necdet Calp, a career civil servant, which was to be the loyal opposition.

Turkey's 1980 coup and its three-year sequel of military rule, therefore, raised this basic question: Would Turkey find its way to full civilian-democratic government, avoiding the past experience of economic and political crises leading to periodic military intervention? Or would the country slip into a dreary alternation of military and quasi-military regimes punctuated by coups and countercoups, a pattern all too familiar in Latin America, the Middle East, and other developing regions? The answer was that Turkey's democratic prospects this time were substantially better than before—in part because of what went according to the generals' plans, and in part because of what went against them.

Not only had the military carried out their coup swiftly and peacefully; they also had brought under control the violence rampant throughout Turkey in the late 1970s by arresting the members of the terrorist networks of left and right. Similarly, the military regime proceeded to round up the vast stores of arms smuggled in by leftists from Bulgaria and Syria or taken by rightists from the army's own depots.

The 1982 constitution, drafted by a civilian assembly convened by the generals, turned out to be overelaborate in many of its details; nevertheless, it created a workable balance between a strong presidency and a cabinet responsible to the elected legislature, the Grand National Assembly of Turkey. Above all, the accompanying electoral law, at long last, encouraged a viable two-party system that was likely to reflect the commitment of six out of seven Turkish voters to gradual and peaceful democratic change. A strong system of government by moderate political parties, in turn, was likely to cope far better with recurrent economic and financial crises than had the deadlocked coalition cabinets of the 1960s and 1970s. This much went according to plan.

By contrast, the clumsy attempt of the military to control both the nature and the personnel of future political parties created needless difficulties for the post-1983 regime. There was an inherent contradiction between the constitutional promise of free debate and democratic choice and the continuing ban on the very parties and politicians that had previously engaged in such debate. Sooner or later, that contradiction

would have tumbled the house of cards so elaborately contrived by the political planners on the military staff. The ban on
politicians previously successful at the polls was bound to
lower the available level of political skills, confuse the emerging
alignments, and make the resulting structure that much more
fragile during the inevitable testing to which others would subject it. Neither in Turkey nor anywhere else is there a stable
midway solution between full freedom of political choice and
full authoritarian control.

The denouement was hastened by the Motherland Party's
resounding election victory of November 1983. Özal's campaign style and TV performance made a lively contrast to the
stodginess of the other, handpicked party leaders; and the majority of voters eagerly rallied to the one party truly independent of the military. In the end, Evren's junta overcame its
bitter disappointment and accepted the voters' verdict with
good grace. By 1986, even the restrictions on political activities
of former leaders had been all but hollowed out. One of them,
Bülent Ecevit, delegated to his wife the task of forming a new
party under a different name. The other, Süleyman Demirel, on
a "nonpolitical" speaking tour and before enthusiastic audiences, took direct exception to President Evren's earlier praise
of the "calm and quiet" restored to the country in 1980: while
"some may find it easier to rule a silent country," his own
preference was for a "talkative" nation.[3]

Turkey's democratic prospects look much brighter than before: law and order have been restored and a workable set of
institutions adopted in principle; and the electorate's good
sense and an ever livelier competition between new and old
leaders are putting the new democratic rules to work regardless
of the restrictions the generals have been trying to impose.

Back to the Barracks: Turkey's Military Tradition

Turkey maintains over 600,000 men under arms, a military
force that, within NATO, is second in size only to that of the
United States. In the non-Communist world, the Turkish system of universal military service is more comprehensive than

any but Israel's or Switzerland's. All able-bodied Turkish males over eighteen are liable to one-and-a-half years of basic training and periodic reserve duty—although the actual length of service will depend on the military's manpower needs at the time.

There is broad agreement throughout Turkish society that such a strong military posture and close ties to the West are essential to the country's national security. Its armed neutrality kept Turkey out of World War II; its continuing military effort and American support have enabled it to defy strong Soviet diplomatic pressures—both at the outset of the Cold War and later as the Arab Middle East became a focus for Moscow's foreign policy. Some of the largest ships that sail under Istanbul's Bosporus Bridge, it must be remembered, are Soviet naval vessels, which, under an international treaty of 1936, ply between the Black Sea and Mediterranean ports, including those of Syria and Libya.

Not only is Turkey's conscription system an essential foundation of foreign policy; it also makes its Ministry of National Defense the country's largest contractor and employer and, all in all, places the armed forces near the center of Turkish society. Six of the seven presidents of the Turkish Republic, beginning with Kemal Atatürk (1923–38) and İsmet İnönü (1938–50) came from a military career.[4] And Turkey's military leaders are proud to invoke the memory of Atatürk, who, having victoriously fought his war to maintain Turkish independence, proclaimed the new nation's commitment to "Peace at home and peace in the world."

In fact, however, Turkey is heir to two distinctive military traditions. One dates to the Ottoman Empire, ruled by a military-administrative establishment, and to the nineteenth-century reforms which put army officers in the vanguard of the movement of Westernization. Atatürk himself was an outstanding product of that reformist military tradition, and the task he undertook in the War of Independence (1919–23) of saving the country from colonial partition was, most immediately, a military task. Civics textbooks and speeches on Turkey's patriotic holidays often invoke Atatürk's appeal to the army to save the country, in its hour of need, from external and internal enemies alike. Military activists thus do not find it hard to argue that Atatürk's national ideology obliges them to decide at what point political division and violence are endangering the national security—and thus to conclude that civilian government can, in effect, continue only at the sufferance of the military high command.

But in Turkey's actual war of national liberation, Atatürk created a truly comprehensive organization including both army personnel and civilians. Indeed, his major political effort went into mobilizing the widest possible spectrum of civilian opinion—urban and rural, religious and secularist, traditional and modern. Following his victory and the proclamation of the Republic, he took off his uniform (except for rare occasions of military ceremony) and insisted on strict separation of military and political affairs—just as, a little later, he was to draw a firm line between government and religion. Specifically, he built his Republican People's Party on the civilian local organizations that had supported the Turkish War of Independence; and forced his associates, as well as opposition leaders, to choose once and for all between military and political careers.

Following that second strand in the Atatürk tradition, his successor, İsmet İnönü, in the late 1940s decided to transform the country's one-party regime in the direction of democracy. His decision was prompted, in part, by immediate pragmatic considerations. Turkey's six years of armed neutrality in World War II had caused much economic hardship and domestic tension, for which the new freedom of expression could serve as a safety valve; and Moscow's postwar military threats made Ankara eager for a rapprochement with the United States and other Western democracies. But domestic and foreign pressures aside, İnönü also believed the time was ripe for implementing more fully Atatürk's populist principles.

Whatever his combination of motives, President İnönü, after some initial hesitation, reconfirmed his decision in 1948, and ultimately showed the courage of his convictions. When the first fully free elections in 1950 overwhelmingly defeated his Republican People's Party, he overcame his resentment at what he felt to be the voters' "ingratitude,"[5] rejected suggestions from military quarters to set aside the election results, and instead resigned his presidency to assume the new task of leader of the opposition in a democratic parliament.

In that same Atatürk-İnönü tradition, the Turkish military junta of 1960–61 under General Cemal Gürsel moved against the minority in its own midst who wished to perpetuate an authoritarian regime—sending Colonel Alpaslan Türkeş and other dissidents into honorable diplomatic exile as military attachés in remote capitals such as Reykjavik and Katmandu. Gürsel and the junta's majority convened a constituent assembly to draw up a new set of more explicit democratic rules, and turned power over to a civilian regime as soon as elections could be held. In the following years, the military stood fully behind that new civilian regime in preventing the plans for two successive coups by another right-wing colonel, Talât Aydemir, who was executed after a full judicial trial in 1964.

After the 1980 coup, General Evren's regime surprised its critics by moving with equal vigor against terrorist organizations of the left and right—the latter led by ex-colonel Türkeş as head of the ultraright Nationalist Action Party and its militant "Grey Wolves." It was again in that Atatürk-İnönü tradition that Evren swallowed his disappointment at the 1983 election returns and began cooperating with Premier Özal, in a pattern that allowed Evren and the generals on the National Security Council to concentrate on issues of internal and external security, and Özal on domestic and international economics.

This much having been said, Turkey's recent military chiefs must be faulted for transferring too readily their lifelong professional habits to the political arena: for overplanning their political maneuvers, seeing the ills of the preceding democratic regimes too narrowly in terms of leaders' personalities, and calling those leaders mercilessly to account, as if by court martial. The 1961 sentence of death by hanging against Prime Minister Adnan Menderes and two of his associates was cruel and excessive by any standard, and it burdened the new democratic regime with a heavy load of resentment. The party which in the 1960s successfully claimed the succession to Menderes's Democrats pointedly called itself the "Justice Party," with clear reference to that injustice at the gallows.

The next military intervention came in 1971, when the country experienced its first major wave of right- and left-wing violence and political assassinations. In contrast to their earlier action, the generals this time decided not to seize power themselves. Instead, through an ultimatum addressed to the parliamentary government and opposition, they forced the appointment of an above-party cabinet acceptable to them. At the same time, the proclamation of martial law in major provinces allowed the military to proceed directly against the left- and right-wing extremists. Nonetheless, following this two-year interlude (1971–73) of what became known as the "coup by memorandum," the parliamentary deadlock and violence grew far worse. By 1980, the military leadership concluded that more rather than less intervention was needed.

Evren's 1980 junta avoided the 1960 junta's mistake of political show trials and death sentences. It was less vindictive, blaming the preceding crisis of deadlock and anarchy on the personalities of Demirel, Ecevit, and their associates—and thus seeking the solution in a sweeping ban on those leaders and their parties.

Turkey's military leaders must take responsibility for many human rights violations against suspects and prisoners in the massive roundups of terrorists and political extremists following the 1971 and 1980 interventions. Above all, any such review of the accomplishments and failures of Turkey's recent military juntas poses all the more sharply the question why military intervention was necessary at all—not just once, but three times in three decades.

Childhood Ills of Democracy

The answer is that Turkey, at the time of its first free and honest election in 1950, was largely, but not entirely, prepared to enter its democratic age. Democracy means self-government by organized disagreement: there must be a tradition of government and a collective sense of self; there must be serious differences—and a structure to contain and resolve them.

Turkey is fortunate in being heir to a strong governmental tradition going back to the early Republic, the nineteenth-century reforms, and beyond that, to the classic Ottoman era. For the Ottoman tradition, often misrepresented as one of arbitrary despotism, was in fact one of government by law and an administration based on broad recruitment, specialized training, and merit advancement. The Turkish Republic inherited most of the personnel of that Ottoman civil service. What became, by the nineteenth century, the fatal flaw of the Ottoman state was the lack of a sense of identity among its citizens, with its religious and linguistic minorities increasingly striving for independence and even its core population unsure whether to think of themselves as Ottomans or as Turks.

As a result of the breakup of the Ottoman Empire, its former Balkan and Arab minorities formed their own states. Within Turkey's new national boundaries of 1923, by contrast, over 90 percent of the people spoke Turkish, and over 98 percent were Muslims. Above all, Turkey's citizens had gained a clear sense of common purpose as a result of Atatürk's bold decision to turn away from the Ottoman past—abandoning any imperial claims, but defending the homeland's frontiers against all comers. Far more than any other "new nation" of the twentieth century, Turkey thus emerged in 1923 with both a tradition of government and a firm sense of self.

Nor was there any shortage of disagreements. Indeed, there was ample fuel for political controversy in the sharp social contrasts between an urban bureaucracy, a rural population of landowners and peasants, and a growing urban working class; the economic opportunities and hardships of a rapidly developing economy; the pressures of the international situation; and even the many personal ambitions released since the late 1940s by electoral competition itself. And of course, once political controversy got under way, long-dormant issues such as religion versus secularism and of the Kurdish ethnic minority in southeastern Turkey were bound to flare up anew.

What Turkey still lacked was a tested structure to contain and resolve such sharpening conflicts—tested institutions, such as those that emerged in European countries through a process of civil war or revolution and reform over the centuries (in England from 1640 to the Victorian age, in France from 1789 to the days of de Gaulle).

In Turkey, the first opposition party had spontaneously appeared as early as 1924, and another, with Atatürk's encouragement, in 1930; yet each of these was dissolved within a few months, well before the next election. In contrast to Atatürk's short-lived experiments at government and opposition, there had been a growing tendency toward intraparty democracy under his successor İnönü—a pattern whereby the Republican People's Party (RPP) left the choice of its parliamentarians and provincial leaders to the rank and file of its local organizations, allowed an increasing range of decisions to its parliamentary caucus, and even permitted the election of a number of independent candidates.

Still, the central feature of an authoritarian one-party regime had remained intact: from 1923 to 1943, the RPP had won every election unopposed, and the newly elected parliamentarians every four years had unanimously reconfirmed their leader as president of the Republic. In sum, the democratic provisions of the 1923 constitution and election law had remained mostly on paper without any test of their practical import. A quarter-century of unchallenged rule had given Atatürk's and İnönü's government party a virtual monopoly on political talent and patronage—and no experience in facing public criticism; and the post-1945 opposition parties, except for a few RPP defectors at the top, had no political experience at all.

Even after İnönü's historic decision in mid-1945 in favor of multiparty democracy, his government continued to proceed in contradictory fashion. The president himself seemed ready to withdraw to a position of a neutral head of state. This, in turn, gave greater discretion to other government and party officials who seemed plainly unsympathetic to the democratic experiment—so that the nascent opposition faced much harassment. Thus, the first elections (July 1946) were scheduled more than a year ahead of time so as to catch the opponents unprepared; in some districts the count was less than honest; and although a small group from the newly formed Democrat

Party were seated, the resulting parliament enjoyed no reputation of legitimacy in the increasingly vocal press or among the public at large. It was not until 1948 that İnönü relieved the growing tension by appointing a more liberal cabinet and, touring the country in the company of officials of both major parties, by pledging his government to full impartiality.

This time, the democratic course was followed so scrupulously that the May 1950 elections (see Figure 1), with a spectacular 89 percent participation, brought a resounding defeat for the RPP, prompting İnönü to exchange the presidency for leadership of the opposition.

The glaring disparity that gave the victorious Democrats 86 percent of the National Assembly on the basis of only 53 percent of the vote was due to a legal feature little noticed in the uncontested elections of the one-party era. For a quarter-century Turkish voters had cast their ballots not for individual candidates but for party lists; and until the 1950s these votes were counted in each province under a "winner take all" system similar to that which elects the U.S. presidential electoral college, rather than to the single-member plurality system that produces solid (but much less lopsided) majorities in the House of Representatives.

Whatever the technical reasons, the quasi-dictatorial power implicit in controlling 420 of the 487 National Assembly seats soon went to the head of Adnan Menderes, the new Democrat premier. Thus, before the next election, the government confiscated all the properties of the RPP opposition, including its headquarters building and the printing presses of its daily newspaper, on allegations that *some* of those assets had been diverted from government sources in the quarter-century of single-party rule. A smaller, Islamic opposition group, the Nation Party, was closed outright and, for good measure, its Central Anatolian stronghold gerrymandered away.

The 1954 elections, held under these grossly unfair conditions, gave Menderes's Democrats an even larger majority (57 percent of the national vote and as much as 93 percent of the Assembly seats). And a plane crash in 1955, from which Menderes alone escaped alive, reinforced his sense of miraculous destiny. Soon the Menderes government felt free to step up its pressure on the press and the judiciary and, during the Cyprus crisis of 1955, to incite anti-Greek riots in Istanbul. As Turkey descended into the severe economic crisis of 1958–59, Menderes tried to make a scapegoat of the opposition by encouraging gangs of toughs to break up its rallies and, when the police proved unable to ensure order, called on the military to do so. It was at this point that the armed forces refused to become Menderes's tool of repression, and instead deposed him in the bloodless coup of 1960.

Whereas lopsided majority rule had been the downfall of Turkey's democratic experiment of the 1950s, the 1961 constitution proceeded to create a balance so neat that it soon calcified into a permanent stalemate. The new basic law curbed the Assembly's power with elaborate checks and balances: a senate partly appointed by the president, presidential veto power over legislation, a lengthy list of individual rights enforceable by the courts, and guarantees of judicial independence. In an

Note: Instead of the November 1983 national election, when some parties were still banned, the local elections of February 1984 have been entered. The September 1986 results were those of a national by-election. The blank intervals in 1960–61 and 1980–83 indicate periods of military rule, when no elections were held and parliament was not in session.

The effects of the change in electoral systems are shown in the diagram below. The bars on the left represent the popular vote; those on the right the seats in parliament. Note the vast overrepresentation of the largest party in 1950, and the fragmentation of parties in parliament in 1961. The post-1983 system gives an intermediate result of more accurate but less fragmented representation.

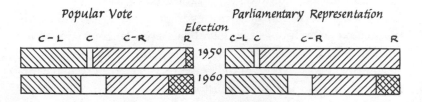

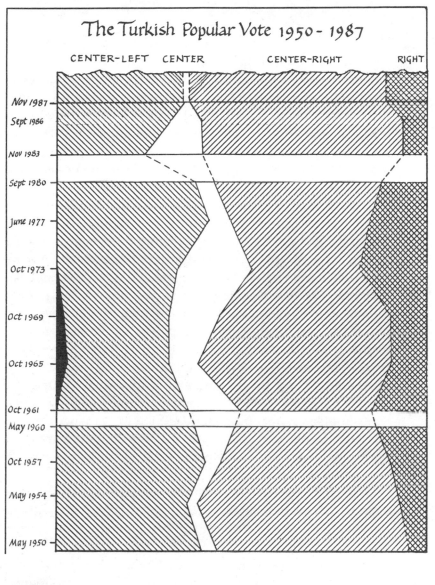

The Turkish Popular Vote 1950 - 1987

CENTER-LEFT   CENTER   CENTER-RIGHT   RIGHT

Nov 1987
Sept 1986
Nov 1983
Sept 1980
June 1977
Oct 1973
Oct 1969
Oct 1965
Oct 1961
May 1960
Oct 1957
May 1954
May 1950

 LEFT: Turkish Labor, 1961–71, 1975–80

 CENTER-LEFT: Republican People's, 1923–80 (İ. İnönü, Ecevit); Social Democratic, 1983–85 (E. İnönü); Social Democratic-Populist, 1985– (E. İnönü); Democratic Left, 1985– (Ecevit)

CENTER: Various splinter parties and independent candidates; parties sponsored by 1980–83 junta; Populist, 1983–86; National Democracy, 1983–86

CENTER RIGHT: Democrat, 1946–60 (Menderes): Justice, 1961–80 (Demirel); Motherland, 1983– (Özal); True Path, 1984– (Demirel)

RIGHT: Nation, 1948–53, 1962–80; Republican Nation, 1954–58; Republican Peasants' Nation, 1958–69 (Türkeş); Nationalist Action, 1969–80 (Türkeş); National Salvation, 1972–80 (Erbakan); Welfare, 1984–

understandable, if excessive, reaction to the lopsided representation of the Menderes period, the constitution makers changed
the election system to a version of proportional representation
(PR).[6] This variety of PR, in due course, produced in Turkey the
same splintering of parties that had paralyzed Weimar Germany
in the 1920s and the French Fourth Republic in the 1950s, and is
creating periodic difficulties for Israel's government.

From 1961 to 1977, Turkey held five elections under this system. Only two of these, in 1965 and 1969, produced a legislative
majority—the winner both times being Süleyman Demirel's
Justice Party. Meanwhile, the number of parties in the Assembly doubled from four in 1961 to eight after 1969. The result was
prolonged deadlocks, intense jockeying among the parties,
caretaker governments without majority support in the Assembly and, at best, fragile coalition cabinets. Of the eight governments in office between 1973 and 1980 (see Table 1), only five
represented majorities in the Grand National Assembly—the
three others being an all-party cabinet appointed to supervise
the 1973 election; a "technocratic" government of civil servants, diplomats, and professors selected to overcome a parliamentary deadlock in the winter of 1974–75; and a minority
government of Ecevit's RPP that failed to obtain a vote of confi-
dence after the 1977 election.

Of the five governments of the 1970s that did enjoy majority
support, two were coalitions of Demirel's Justice Party with the
right-wing National Salvation and Nationalist Action parties.
One of them clung to office for over two years (1975–77) by
avoiding major decisions while the economic situation steadily
deteriorated: it was not uncommon to hear a policy pronouncement by Premier Demirel flatly contradicted the next day by
Deputy Premier Necmettin Erbakan of the NSP. The other
avoided parliamentary defeat for six months (July–December
1977), mostly by preventing a parliamentary quorum.

Two other governments were formed by Bülent Ecevit and
his RPP, the first in coalition with Erbakan's Salvationists (January–September 1974). This incongruous combination of secularist social democrats and Islamic-conservatives was held
together mainly by its activist policy on the Cyprus question.

Table 1. Turkish Cabinets Since 1950

Formed	Prime Minister	Political Circumstances and Support
5/22/50	Adnan Menderes (DP)	DP cabinets based on Assembly majorities in three elections (1950, 408:79; 1954, 490:45; 1957, 419:183)
5/28/60	Gen. Cemal Gürsel	"Committee of National Unity," installed by military coup, deposes and tries Menderes; election under new constitution produces no majority.
11/20/61	İsmet İnönü (RPP)	Coalition of rival RPP and JP formed under pressure from outgoing military
6/25/62	İsmet İnönü (RPP)	Majority coalition of RPP and two minor parties (NTP, RPNP)
12/25/63	İsmet İnönü (RPP)	RPP minority cabinet
1/20/65	Suat Hayri Ürgüplü	Nonpartisan cabinet to supervise 1965 election
10/27/65	Süleyman Demirel (JP)	JP majority cabinets, reconstituted after 1969 election victory and temporary defection of forty-one JP deputies in February 1970 budget vote
3/26/71	Nihat Erim	Nonpartisan cabinet installed by military ("coup by memorandum"), reshuffled after eleven ministers defect in December, resigns when Assembly refuses emergency powers
5/22/72	Ferit Melen	After seven-week crisis, new nonpartisan cabinet negotiated between president and parties in Assembly
4/15/73	Naim Talu	Nonpartisan cabinet to supervise October 1973 election; continued as attempts at RPP, JP, and RPP-JP cabinets fail
1/25/74	Bülent Ecevit (RPP)	After four-month cabinet crisis, RPP-NSP coalition wins 233:217 majority
11/17/74	Sadi Irmak	Nonpartisan (bureaucratic) cabinet loses confidence vote but continues as caretaker
3/21/75	Süleyman Demirel (JP)	Four-party coalition (JP, NSP, NAP, RRP) wins narrow (222:218) confidence vote, but loses 1977 election
6/21/77	Bülent Ecevit (RPP)	Front runner in election, but twelve votes short of majority, RPP loses confidence vote
7/21/77	Süleyman Demirel (JP)	Three-party coalition (JP, NSP, NAP) wins 229:219 confidence vote, but loses majority as eleven JP deputies defect
1/5/78	Bülent Ecevit (RPP)	RPP forms cabinet of record size (including nine posts for JP defectors, three for minor parties) to gain eleven-vote margin in 229:218 confidence vote; resigns after by-election
11/12/79	Süleyman Demirel (JP)	JP minority cabinet, with initial support of smaller parties, avoids confronting Assembly as presidential elections deadlock and violence soars
9/21/80	Adm. Bülend Ulusu	Installed after "National Unity Committee" seizes power in military coup of September 12
12/13/83	Turgut Özal (MP)	Installed after MP wins 211:188 majority in November election; defections from military-sponsored parties boost its majority to 237:162 (October 1986)

Key to Party Abbreviations

DP	= Democrat Party (Menderes)	NTP	= New Turkey Party
JP	= Justice Party (Demirel)	RPNP	= Republican Peasants' Nation Party
MP	= Motherland Party (Ozal)	RPP	= Republican People's Party
NAP	= Nationalist Action Party (Türkeş)		(İnönü, Ecevit)
NSP	= National Salvation Party (Erbakan)	RRP	= Republican Reliance Party

The other was a cabinet of unprecedented size formed by Ecevit in 1978, with twelve ministries going to defectors from the Justice Party or members of minor parties, who, among them, guaranteed him a slender majority of eleven.

Finally, when some of those defectors redefected the following year, Demirel in October 1979 formed a minority government of the Justice Party with outside support from the smaller right-wing parties. It was under this administration that Turgut Özal prepared his austerity plan of January 1980 so as to restore Turkey's creditworthiness with the IMF and multinational banks; and generally, the single-party minority government dealt more successfully with economic issues than could a multiparty coalition.

Still, Demirel's relations with the parliament remained precarious. When the time came to elect a new president, the legislators remained hopelessly deadlocked in more than one hundred ballots taken over a six-month period; and once again some of the parties sabotaged the legislative work by preventing a quorum. Demirel himself seemed to feel little urgency in filling the presidency since the vacancy enabled a member of his own Justice Party, as presiding officer of the Senate, to act as interim president. Although Turkey was beginning to resolve its foreign payments crisis, domestic inflation ran at an annual rate of more than 100 percent, and by the summer of 1980, political violence throughout the nation began to cost an average of up to thirty lives a day. This, in brief, was the setting that prompted the military intervention of September 1980.

Turkish Political Parties: The Solid Center

Aside from the periodic military interludes, the Turkish political scene since the late 1940s has been dominated by the political parties. The major ones among these, like those of the United States, have a broad-based appeal and a pragmatic, flexible approach; whereas some of the minor parties are more ideologically oriented: Islamic-conservative, ultranationalist, or militant socialist. All Turkish parties, major and minor alike, follow the Western European pattern of dues-paying membership and local organizations down to the county, small town, or city district level. Their centralized national organizations hold periodic party congresses and adopt detailed official programs. The leadership of each national party sits in the parliament, with the chairman its automatic candidate for the prime ministership.

As in other European countries, there are legal provisions that bar direct party activity of civil servants and otherwise put some distance between parties and the bureaucracy. Under the coalition governments of the 1970s, however, some of the parties found ways to circumvent those rules by patronage appointments or preferential promotions in the ministries assigned to them.[7]

Every Turkish party has its pictorial symbol, flown as a flag from national or provincial headquarters, and occasionally worn as a lapel button. One important incidental function of such symbols has been to help the illiterate voter pick the proper ballot from the piles in the curtained voting booth to place into the official envelope and cast into the box. The oldest of those party symbols is the six arrows (white and radiating upward in a field of red) of the Republican People's Party, adopted in 1935 to symbolize Atatürk's principles of republicanism, nationalism, populism, secularism, revolutionism, and *étatisme*.[8] In the 1960s, the Justice Party put on its banner a prancing horse, the National Salvation Party a key, and the Turkish Labor Party a cogwheel and blade of wheat (to symbolize its leftist appeal to workers and peasants). More recently, Özal's Motherland Party has campaigned under the symbol of a beehive built into a map of Turkey. The Social Democrats started out with a symbol of an olive branch and, after their merger with the Populists in 1985, adopted an emblem of six rays (reminiscent of the old Republican People's Party's six arrows) surrounded by two olive branches.

The pattern of popular support and political alignment among Turkish parties developed logically from the late 1940s. The RPP, during a quarter-century of single-party rule, had built up its network of support from the bureaucracy in Ankara and the provinces, prominent families in the rural districts, and economic interests favored by the inward-oriented policy of *étatisme*. In contrast, the Democrat Party (DP), founded in 1946, presented itself as the champion of private enterprise, attracting strong support from large merchants, industrialists, and cash-crop farmers; and from local families or factions in opposition to the dominant RPP-affiliated groups. But the DP also attracted vocal support in those early years from journalists, who had long chafed under the media censorship of the one-party regime, and urban intellectuals welcoming the country's progress toward democracy.

This alignment shifted somewhat over the years. The Democrats, in the late 1950s, solidified their commercial and agrarian support but antagonized their intellectual sympathizers[9] through high-handed dealing with the opposition; and by the early 1970s, Ecevit tried to move the RPP toward a democratic socialist program that would appeal more strongly to organized labor, some of the poorer regions of the country, and leftist intellectuals.

The resulting lineup of Turkey's major parties has closely resembled that of Republicans versus Democrats in the United States, Conservatives versus Labor in Britain, or Christian Democrats versus Social Democrats in West Germany. Menderes's Democrats, Demirel's Justice Party, and most recently Özal's Motherland Party have broadly occupied the right-of-center position—with Demirel's True Path Party emerging as a rival claimant by 1986. At the left of center there has been the Republican People's Party under İsmet İnönü and then Ecevit—and since 1985 the newly unified Social Democratic-Populist Party under Erdal İnönü.

Turkish election campaigns since the 1950s also have offered many features familiar from the United States and other democracies—attention to the personalities of leaders and their rivalries, charges of corruption and specific abuses, and promises of redress of grievances. Turkey's national newspapers, such as *Hürriyet*, *Milliyet*, *Tercüman*, *Günaydın*, and *Cumhuriyet*, are published simultaneously in Istanbul, Ankara, and other major centers (the first three even in West Germany for the benefit of Turkish guest workers). As in America, most newspapers are not clearly identified with a political party. Instead, their active competition for readership and advertising has given most of them a strident, sensationalist tone. Sex and terrorism, along with more conventional news, thus often emerge as the chief front-page subjects—the notable exception in recent years being the sober reporting and analysis of the left-of-center *Cumhuriyet*.

Remarkably, in Turkish general elections, the voting participation has been far higher than it is in the United States or even in many European democracies—as much as 89 percent in the first fully free election in 1950, averaging 76 percent for the entire 1950–80 period, and never dropping below 64 percent.[10] From the start of Turkey's democratic era, ordinary Turkish citizens have been deeply convinced that national elections and their individual ballots make a difference—and only a minority of them flagged in that conviction during the days of deadlock, violence, and terror in the 1970s.

In the nationwide political contest, the personal element has always been prominent. İsmet İnönü and Celâl Bayar, who faced each other as leaders of the RPP and the DP in 1950, had been political rivals since the days of Atatürk; and the name of the Justice Party, as noted earlier, implied a bitter protest against the hanging of ex-premier Menderes by General Gürsel's military regime. The national elections of the 1960s and 1970s turned into acrimonious contests between Bülent Ecevit of the RPP—poet, journalist, and eloquent spokesman for the grievances of the lower class, and Süleyman Demirel of the JP—the engineer and "father of dams" with his broad regional dialect and conservative, pashalike touch. In 1983, the Motherland Party owed its victory, as already noted, in no small part to Turgut Özal's plain looks and zestful, unflappable performances on television and at election rallies. The very name of Erdal İnönü, İsmet İnönü's son, served as a rallying point for the Social Democratic-Populist party as it became the major center-left opposition in the mid-1980s. And Süleyman Demirel, although banned from official political activity, emerged as the de facto leader of the True Path Party and charismatic rival to Turgut Özal for the leadership of the center-right.

The mainstream of Turkish political debate, comprising the major center-right and center-left parties and centrist splinter parties, thus has typically concentrated on leaders and specific (perhaps ephemeral) issues, and conversely steered clear of ideology. In this important respect, Turkey differs from the continental European model with its Christian Democratic, Socialist, and Communist parties—not to mention the Israeli precedent of parties based on intensely shaded varieties of socialism, Zionism, or religious orthodoxy. Rather, the Turkish pattern resembles that of the United States with its national alliances of regional and local groupings devoted not to abstract principle but, concretely, to more progressive or conservative social policies. Perhaps it was no coincidence that Turkey's early national elections were fought out between groups calling themselves the Republican People's and Democrat parties.

A partial exception to this rule of broadly based and non-ideological major parties was the adoption by the RPP of a democratic socialist program under Ecevit's leadership after 1972. Even here, political circumstances forced a more pragmatic approach—including Ecevit's coalition government in 1974 with the right-wing, Islamicist Salvation Party. The bulk of the RPP organization, moreover, never came to share Ecevit's more militant ideological approach. That rift came out in the open after 1983, as most of the RPP organization joined Erdal İnönü's Social Democratic Party, whereas Ecevit and his wife saw their rival Democratic Left Party off to a slow start. The Social Democrats, campaigning under their olive branch symbol, advocated social justice and income redistribution within a mixed public-private economy; and this moderate tendency in the main opposition party was further reinforced by the Social Democratic-Populist merger in 1985.

These basic alignments among the major parties have remained remarkably stable despite intervening military coups, changes in constitutional rules, or bans on former parties and politicians. When Menderes's Democrat Party was dissolved by the 1960 junta, two separate groups emerged to claim its heritage in the 1961 election, but by 1965 the Justice Party (JP), under Süleyman Demirel's leadership, clearly had won over the rival New Turkey Party. In addition, as a result of the party-splintering tendencies inherent in the election system of the Second Republic, two smaller centrist groups split off from the major parties, the Reliance Party of 1967–80 and the Democratic Party of 1970–80, representing initially the disappointed ambition of one of Ecevit's and one of Demirel's rivals for major-party leadership. Still, even during the worst party splintering of the Second Republic, at least three out of four Turkish voters typically cast their ballots for one of the two major parties—whose combined vote averaged 91 percent in the 1950s, and 74 percent in the 1960s and 1970s.

In the 1983 elections, it was not the officially favored Nationalist Democracy Party of General Sunalp but Turgut Özal's late-entry Motherland Party which successfully claimed most of the JP's former voters—although that claim was soon challenged by Demirel's own True Path Party. The merger in 1985 of the Social Democratic and Populist parties reconstituted a center-left movement ready to occupy the slot of the former Republican People's Party. Despite all the vicissitudes of recent Turkish party life, the vast majority of voters have continuously grouped and regrouped themselves into the two major parties to the right and left of center.

The Political Fringe: Ideology and Terror

The ideological motifs, nonetheless, have appeared on the political fringes outside the major parties. The first of these smaller groups was the Nation Party, founded in 1948, whose appeal was mainly to Islamic-conservative sentiment, with its main stronghold in a central Anatolian region that had been the traditional center of the Bektaşi order.

The Nation Party and later Islamic-conservative groups faced the constitutional and legal provisions prohibiting the advocacy of an Islamic caliphate and generally protecting secularism. Interpreted stringently, these were used to ban the Nation Party in 1953—which was reorganized almost immediately, under a slightly modified program and leadership, as the "Republican Nation Party" (1954). Still, the Nation Party in these two incarnations increased its vote only slowly, from 3 percent in 1950 to 7 percent in 1957.

A better showing was made by the National Salvation Party (NSP), founded in 1972 by Necmettin Erbakan, an engineer with a graduate degree from West Germany, whose rhetoric emphasized that Islam was the most modern of the world's religions and fully compatible with advanced technology. Erbakan had made a name for himself as the champion of provincial merchants against the dominant influence of the large Istanbul-based corporations over Turkey's chambers of commerce, and in their first election contest in the fall of 1973, Erbakan's Salvationists secured a remarkable 11.8 percent. In matters of foreign policy, he supported the 1974 military intervention on Cyprus. More broadly, he argued that Turkey, as a Muslim country, should withdraw from its "unnatural" association with the European Economic Community, and instead join an Islamic Common Market of the future. Yet when Erbakan, with much publicity, visited Riyad, he met with a distinctly cool reception from the ever-cautious Saudi leadership.

In the perennial political stalemate of the 1970s, Erbakan parlayed the NSP's third-party status into government coalitions first with Ecevit's RPP (1974) and then with Demirel's JP (1975–77, 1977–78). Nonetheless, even under those most favorable circumstances, and in the polarized political climate of the 1970s, the NSP's vote declined from its 1973 high of nearly 12 percent to only 8.5 percent in 1977, with its parliamentary seats cut by more than half, from forty-nine to twenty-four. In September 1980, the refusal of NSP members at a rally in the city of Konya to sing the national anthem outraged wide segments of Turkish sentiment, and indeed furnished the immediate provocation that prompted General Evren's coup. The NSP, too, has been under indictment for violating the secularist, anticaliphate provisions of the law, but was subsequently acquitted. By 1984, the NSP's place as champion of Islamic traditionalism was taken by the newly formed Welfare Party—which polled no more than 4.8 percent in the local elections of that year and only 5.6 percent in the national by-elections of 1986.

Erbakan's Salvationists were clearly at odds with the main trend of Turkey's secularism, mutual tolerance, and orientation to the West. Nonetheless, it is important to guard against the fallacy of outside observers that would classify them with the followers of Iran's Khomeini under the loose label of "Islamic fundamentalism." Iran is a Shiite-Muslim and Turkey a Sunni-Muslim country, and the Sunni-Shiite split goes back to the earliest days of Islam. Hence Turkish religious-conservative groups such as Erbakan's NSP, being emphatically Sunni in orientation, feel little attraction to any regime of Shiite ayatollahs.

Two other ideological tendencies have played an even lesser role in electoral politics than has Islamic conservatism. One of these is the ultranationalism of the Nationalist Action Party, founded in 1969 by Alpaslan Türkeş, former leader of the authoritarian minority of the 1960–61 junta. The party espoused the ideal of a corporate state at home and the policy of pan-Turkism abroad—that is, the utopia of political unification of Turkey with the Turkic-speaking populations of Soviet Central Asia and Western China. The NAP's nationwide vote rose from 3 percent in 1969 and 1973 to a maximum of 6 percent in 1977. And its militant youth organization of "Grey Wolves" became a major force on the terrorist scene of the 1970s until crushed by the military after 1980. It is this combination of corporatism, irredentism, and uniformed militancy which, in the eyes of its critics, marked the NAP as a protofascist movement.

The other extremist tendency is revolutionary Marxism-Leninism of the Soviet variety, which in Turkey has been represented by the Turkish Labor Party (TLP). The TLP had briefly obtained enough of a following to gain 3 percent of the popular vote and fifteen parliamentary seats in 1965. In 1969 it was reduced to only two seats, and by 1973 the shift of the Republican People's Party toward democratic socialism completely undercut the electoral appeal of the far left.

Closed down by court order from 1971 to 1973, the TLP never did recover from its own multiple splits. In 1975, it failed to meet the electoral requirement of organization in fifteen provinces in time for the Senate elections. In the Assembly elections of 1977, it did qualify, but won only 0.1 percent. The groups that split off, under names such as the Socialist Labor Party, the Workers' Party of Turkey, or the Socialist Party, did even less well and hence were unable to enter any electoral contests.

The major significance of both pan-Turkish extremism and communism in Turkish politics was outside the electoral and parliamentary process. Marxism found a stronghold in DISK (Turkish acronym for the Confederation of Revolutionary Trade Unions), which split off from the mainstream Turkish Labor Confederation (TÜRKİŞ) in 1967, and intermittently in the 1970s tried to organize political strikes and violent May Day demonstrations. Marxist ideology in its Stalinist, Maoist, and even Albanian versions proved popular in the 1970s among certain urban strata, and particularly among some teachers and many students on university campuses. The growing paralysis of the governmental system encouraged the growth of left-wing and right-wing terrorism in cities and towns throughout Turkey.

By the early 1970s, these groups developed a regular network of arms supply, those to the leftists smuggled overland from Bulgaria or Syria or through Turkey's lengthy Black Sea coast, and those to the rightists obtained in return for drug smuggling or leaked to the Nationalist Action Party by friendly elements in the armed forces. Thus, in 1977, thirty-seven people were killed at the May Day demonstrations when right-wingers or, as Maoist groups alleged, Moscow-oriented DISK members opened fire on the crowd of moderate unionists.

The appeal of rightist and leftist extremes was especially powerful among Turks in their late teens who faced the almost certain prospect of unemployment in times of economic crisis—and who made attractive recruits, since Turkish criminal law is particularly lenient with suspects under twenty-one. Turkish universities, with their huge, overcrowded lecture halls and lack of close contact between faculty and students, had always been centers of ideological debate and, by the late 1970s, became hotbeds of terrorism.

In the ethnically or religiously mixed portions of the country, those distinctions quickly transformed themselves into violent gang warfare. Thus the rioting that in December 1978 claimed 117 people killed and over 1,000 wounded in Turkey's southeastern town of Kahramanmaraş appears to have erupted from tensions and competition for scarce jobs among Sunnis and Alevis, and Turks and Kurds, some of them old residents and others recent migrants from the countryside. And in July 1980, the police and army cracked down on the town of Fatsa, on Turkey's Black Sea coast, where local extremists of the left had defied the Ankara authorities by proclaiming their rule of "people's committees."

How readily the small minority of disaffected young men could drift toward radicalism of either right or left is strikingly illustrated by the career of Mehmed Ali Ağca, the would-be assassin of Pope John Paul II in 1981. In his late teens he had joined the terrorist Grey Wolves of the Nationalist Movement Party, and in 1979 he had been jailed for the assassination of Abdi İpekçi, editor of *Milliyet* and Turkey's leading liberal journalist of the day. Escaping from jail through his right-wing connections, Ağca apparently spent some months among the Turkish guest workers in Germany, and with the opium- and weapons-smuggling gangs operating the route from Turkey through Communist Bulgaria and Yugoslavia to Western Europe. Eventually (according to one widespread theory), he was recruited into cooperating with the Bulgarian secret service in carrying out the plot against the Pope.

In parliamentary elections, the maximum vote obtained by Turkish Marxists was their initial 3 percent (1965). On the extreme right, the Nationalist Action Party (NAP) started out at that same level in 1969 and by 1977 doubled its vote to 6.4 percent. Like the Islamic NSP, the NAP found its power and respectability enhanced by its inclusion in coalition cabinets of the late 1970s. Thus, while in 1975–77, Türkeş's group had to content itself with a deputy premiership and a post of "minister of state," in 1977–78 it also gained control of the ministries of commerce, health, and customs—the latter of particular importance, presumably, for facilitating protection of arms- and drug-smuggling gangs.

Neither the extreme left nor the extreme right ever was able to match the voting performance of the Islamic conservatives. But even if the votes for Erbakan's NSP and the Alevi-oriented Unity Party are added to the extreme right and left vote, the total for all the nondemocratic and antidemocratic parties still remains narrowly limited—14 percent in 1961, 12 percent in 1965 and 1969, a maximum of 17 percent in 1973, and a slight decline to 16 percent in 1977.

These figures have two important implications, one immediate and the other long-term. In the 1973–80 Assemblies, the few seats held by the NSP and NAP often were enough to swing the balance between the two major parties, and hence became the lever for exacting exorbitant concessions. Worse, the prolonged, cynical haggling often would immobilize legislative activity altogether. The resulting governmental paralysis would discredit the democratic process, encourage political activists to resort to street violence instead—and prevent the enfeebled government from coping with the resulting wave of terrorism without calling in the military or being displaced by them.

Factors such as Turkey's long tradition of military service and the social tensions generated by unemployment and internal migration, no doubt, made their contributions to the Turkish climate of violence. Yet there can be little question that the most important single factor in the decay of Turkish democracy in the 1970s was the divisive electoral system of proportional representation. For it was electoral fragmentation that paralyzed the Ankara legislature; made the government powerless in the face of mounting terror and anarchy throughout the country; and in both ways placed maximum power in the very hands of those small ultraright, communist, or Islamic-conservative groups with minimal attachment to the democratic process.

The second, converse implication of all this is of crucial importance for the longer-term future. The firm commitment of the vast majority of Turkish voters to the centrist, democratic parties of the mainstream constitutes the most impressive single feature of Turkey's recent political life. In eight successive elections over three decades—including a period of parliamentary paralysis and rampant terrorism—between 83 and 97 percent of the electorate, or at least six Turkish voters out of seven, have voted decisively for gradual democratic change.

What Turkey desperately needed in those darkest days of the late 1970s was a constitutional and parliamentary mechanism to translate such sound political sense among the voters throughout the nation into effective democratic government in Ankara. The 1982 constitution and election law, and the accommodation between President Evren and Prime Minister Özal since 1983, have at last begun to provide that essential requirement. For as we noted earlier, the suppression of the double wave of terrorism, and the collection of the vast amounts of small arms that had accumulated in private hands, has been one of the major achievements of the Evren regime of 1980–83. And Özal's Motherland Party has helped Turkey overcome the parliamentary paralysis and frustration that was the other major source of the extremism and terror of the 1970s.

Five

The Turkish-American Alliance: Foundations and Strains

Ankara's Diplomacy: Beyond Hitler's Promises and Stalin's Threats

Changes on the Turkish domestic scene have often been profound, as politics has shifted from authoritarianism toward democracy, from party responsibility to parliamentary deadlock or unstable coalitions, from civilian government to interludes of military rule, or from endemic terrorism to renewed stability. In contrast to such frequent internal changes, Ankara's foreign policy has displayed remarkable continuity. Indeed, Turkey's external relations have been marked by a long-term perspective, a sense of responsibility, and a realism found in few developing nations and far from universal even among the democracies of the West.

In Turkey's increasingly democratic atmosphere, there have, of course, been disagreements—at times even sharp controversies—over specific aspects of those foreign relations. Ankara governments of the late 1940s and the 1950s were enthusiastic in forging Turkey's links with the West; yet by the 1960s, wide segments of opinion turned sharply critical of the United States over Cyprus and other issues; and by the 1970s, vocal minorities sought rapprochement with the Muslim countries of the Middle East and even the Soviet Union.

Among the major political parties, nonetheless, it has been taken for granted that politics, no matter how bitterly fought at home, stops at the water's edge. As a leading British observer

84

recently put it, "On most foreign policy issues, there is nor-
mally a broad consensus of opinion across most of the Turkish
political spectrum."[1] The career officials who staff the Turkish
foreign ministry and its overseas missions are the most highly
trained, internationally oriented, and elitist part of the government establishment. In contrast to Washington's practice, major embassies are not used as rewards for political friends or
financial supporters of an incoming government, but rotated
among senior foreign service officers.[2] Since the earliest days of
the Ankara government, foreign ministers have maintained an
average tenure in office of nearly two-and-a-half years—longer
than prime ministers, and half again as long as their other
cabinet colleagues.[3]

This continuity of foreign policy has survived the ever more
intense partisan controversies since the 1960s. Even under
weak coalition governments, as in the 1970s, it was taken for
granted that the post of foreign minister would be held by a
respected figure from one of the major centrist parties and that
details of policy would be shaped by career officials.[4] After
1980, both the military government and Ozal's Motherland
Party cabinet entrusted the foreign portfolio directly to ranking
career diplomats: İlter Türkmen, previously ambassador to
Athens and the United Nations and general secretary of the
Foreign Ministry; and Vahit Halefoğlu, former ambassador to
Moscow, Bonn, and other key posts—both of them alumni of
Galatasaray and the Mülkiye.

Not surprisingly, there is a pervasive sense among Turkey's
foreign policy makers that international commitments extend
beyond changes in party government or even constitutional
regime, and that international treaties are to be scrupulously
observed. The newly organized Turkish nationalist movement,
in its victorious War of Independence (1919–23), claimed only
those territories that the preceding Ottoman regime had retained in the armistice of 1918, which sealed its final defeat in
World War I;[5] and under the peace treaty of 1923, the newly
established Republic of Turkey paid off its agreed share of the
Ottoman international debt. Turkey has proved immune to the
public wrangles between executive and legislature that afflict

the process of foreign policy making in Washington, let alone the abrupt shifts in foreign relations that often accompany changes of regime in Third World nations.

It is within this nonpartisan, professional framework of foreign policy that Turkish leaders have sought to reconcile the apparent contradictions in the country's geographic position and historic heritage. Turkey is one of the few developing countries never to have become a European colony—and a new nation that after its victorious War of Independence launched its own most ambitious program of Westernization. In contrast to the almost continual warfare that marked the history of the Ottoman Empire,[6] the Turkish Republic has now been at peace for over sixty years. Turkey stayed out of World War II only to become the first diplomatic battleground in the subsequent "Cold War"; and ever since the 1950s, it has been the NATO ally with the longest direct frontier with the Soviet Union. Today Turkey is a nation with strong democratic commitments; it is a participating member in NATO, OECD, the Council of Europe, and the Islamic Conference Organization—and it interposes a solid barrier between the Soviet Union and the turbulent Middle East.

For all its elements of continuity and synthesis, Ankara's foreign policy has been far from static. Indeed, the formulas by which Turkey's leaders and foreign service officers reconciled those factors of geography and history have undergone several major revisions. The most notable shift, of course, was that from the desperate retreat and defense of the theocratic Ottoman Empire to the peaceable steadfastness of Atatürk's Westernizing nation-state. Of equal import was the shift in the late 1940s from the earlier neutrality to Turkey's determined stand against Soviet expansion and toward alliance with the West. A further, subtler shift may be in the making in the 1980s, as Turkey more consciously assumes its role as a cultural and commercial bridge between Europe and the Middle East.

The Turkish Republic in its original frontiers of 1923 was a neighbor of Greece and Bulgaria in the West and of the Soviet Union and Iran in the East. To the south, the new nation bordered on colonial dependencies of each of the major European imperial powers, including Britain's mandate in Iraq, France's mandate in Syria, and the Dodecanese islands in the Aegean Sea, which were an Italian colony between the world wars. In this complex environment, Atatürk's abandonment of the centuries-old pattern of Ottoman belligerence involved not only strict observance of existing agreements, but also a conscious decision to settle outstanding disputes by mutual concession and peaceful diplomacy.

A disputed boundary in the northeast was adjusted in Turkey's favor by a friendship treaty with the newly consolidated Soviet regime in 1921—the first such pact for Ankara and (along with those with Iran and Afghanistan) for Moscow as well. Conversely, Turkey in 1926 accepted a League of Nations decision awarding the disputed, oil-rich Mosul region to Iraq. Another boundary adjustment occurred in 1938–39, as France, on behalf of its Syrian mandate, agreed to let the border district of Alexandrette (or, in Turkish, Hatay), with its Turkish-speaking majority, vote for merger with Turkey—a measure never recognized by independent Syria, whose postage stamps continued to show Alexandrette as Syrian.

Atatürk's crowning foreign policy achievement remained the 1930 friendship pact with the Greek government of Eleutherios Venizelos, the very leader who had launched the invasion which Atatürk's nationalist troops had halted a decade earlier on the outskirts of Ankara. By 1934 this Greek-Turkish agreement was expanded into a Balkan Pact with Yugoslavia and Romania, which sought to preserve stability in that volatile region on the eve of Hitler's aggression.

In the turbulent environment of the late 1930s and early 1940s, Turkey's policy was single-mindedly dedicated to preserving its independence and integrity. The threat posed by the Nazi-Soviet Pact of August 1939 prompted Ankara to conclude a Treaty of Mutual Assistance with London and Paris.[7] Yet when the defeat of France, the German invasion of the Balkans, and the failure of the British military expedition in support of Greece (April 1941) led to the collapse of Allied plans in the eastern Mediterranean, Ankara persisted in its cautious neutrality—a stance abandoned only formally in 1944 and 1945, as the war's outcome was assured.[8]

Adolf Hitler himself paid grudging tribute to Ankara's armed neutrality and firm dedication to the status quo. Having just occupied much of Eastern Europe, in part by offering countries such as Hungary or Bulgaria generous chunks of their neighbors' territory, he found himself thwarted in pushing that tactic into the Middle East—and thereby winning a possibly decisive victory over Britain, which at the time was his sole military antagonist. "Turkey would not even like the promise of Syria," the exasperated Führer complained—noting realistically that distances, the mountainous terrain, and Turkish military strength ruled out the "possibility of attempting the Operation" across Turkey and into Syria and Iraq "by force."[9]

When others did threaten Turkey's integrity, the peaceful stance changed to solid defiance, or even belligerence. Thus Moscow early in 1945 demanded, as its price for renewing the Soviet-Turkish friendship treaty of 1921, that Turkey surrender its northeastern districts of Kars and Ardahan and arrange for a "joint defense" of the Turkish Straits—this last clearly a euphemism for Soviet naval bases on the vital Bosporus and Dardanelles. Turkey's response was unequivocal: "We are under no obligation to give up Turkish soil or Turkish rights to anyone," President İnönü assured an applauding National Assembly. "We shall live with honor and die with honor." And the Assembly speaker coupled his plea for renewed Soviet-Turkish friendship with a firm warning: "Kars is the key to the gate of the Mediterranean, the only barrier to a big inundation. . . .If the Russians insist on their demand, we shall fight to the last Turk."[10]

It was no coincidence that Turkey was to become the first diplomatic arena of the incipient Cold War. Most countries of Eastern and Central Europe had been actual battlegrounds in World War II; hence in planning the military operations for Hitler's defeat, Russia and the Western powers were obliged to delineate clearly their respective zones of military occupation—and hence of postwar control. Turkey's neutrality, by contrast, had left its future status ambiguous, and thus made it a tempting target for Stalin's postwar expansionism. The result was that Turkey's leaders as early as 1945 felt compelled to state their own policy of containment—a stance that Washington over the following years backed up with acts such as the Istanbul visit of the battleship U.S.S. *Missouri* in April 1946 and the proclamation of the Truman Doctrine in 1947.

Cold War and Truman Doctrine

It was fortunate for Turkey that the United States came to assume leadership in rallying Western resistance to the Soviet threat. The European powers for centuries had been involved in their imperial scramble to divide or preserve the sultans' legacy. By contrast, Turkish opinion had come to respect the United States for the educational and medical efforts of its missionaries, for President Wilson's championship of national self-determination, and for the principles of a just international order proclaimed in the Atlantic Charter of 1941.

Caught up in their own confrontation with the Soviets, Turkish leaders were glad that Washington did not relapse into isolationism or remain content with the enunciation of mere principles. On March 12, 1947, President Truman's statement to Congress rang out loud and clear:

> At the present moment in world history nearly every nation must choose between alternative ways of life. . . .One way of life is based upon the will of the majority. . . .The second way of life is based upon the will of a minority forcibly imposed upon the majority. . . .I believe that it must be the policy of the United States to support free peoples who are resisting attempted subjugation by armed minorities or by outside pressure. I believe that we must assist free peoples to work out their own destinies in their own way. . . .I, therefore, ask the Congress to provide authority for assistance to Greece and Turkey.

Truman's forthright commitment soon turned the tide throughout the Mediterranean and Middle Eastern regions. On Turkey's eastern border, the Shah's Iranian government finished off a secessionist Communist regime in Azerbaijan. To the west, Tito's Yugoslavia defected from the Stalinist camp to neutralism, and the royal Greek government by 1948 was winning the civil war against communist guerrillas.

Above all, Washington's backing for Turkey's own resolute stand prompted Moscow to pursue its aims with greater caution—and to turn its attention to locations such as Berlin, Korea, Vietnam, and Cuba; or in the Middle East, to Arab countries such as Egypt, Iraq, and Syria. Remarkably, by the midfifties, Moscow and Ankara had "normalized" relations to the point of making plans for a joint hydroelectric dam on the very frontier so hotly disputed in 1945. Since the 1960s, Moscow's policy toward Ankara has combined correct, or even friendly, diplomacy and international economic aid with subversive radio propaganda—as well as encouragement of "revolutionary" trade unions and intellectual "peace movements" within Turkey, and of Armenian and Kurdish terrorist organizations from without.

The period from 1947 to the early 1960s was one of almost full convergence of American and Turkish policies. Turkey had found the strong outside support needed to resist the Soviets over the long haul; and American policymakers, eager to line up reluctant nations in Europe or Asia for defensive pacts such as NATO and SEATO, found the Turks an enthusiastic ally. When American forces came to the aid of South Korea in 1950, Turkey was among the few countries to respond eagerly to the UN's call for troops; and its foreign minister, Professor Fuad Köprülü, justified the step with what remains a classic statement of the case for collective security: "If I do not give help today, how can I dare ask the United Nations for help when I am in need of it tomorrow?" For its part, Washington strongly supported, over some European objections, the admission of Greece and Turkey to NATO, completed in 1952.

Turkey's leaders had strongly preferred to be included in Washington's defense plans for Europe, where commitments were likely to prove more durable than on a rapidly shifting Middle Eastern scene; and where the Marshall Plan was under way well before Truman announced his Point Four program of aid to developing countries. On a psychological level, moreover, inclusion in the Marshall Plan for European recovery and, later, the Atlantic Alliance reassured Turkish leaders that the new nation, in its centuries-long journey of "going West," had at last arrived and been accepted.

From the early days of the Cold War, Ankara's and Washington's strategic analysts were agreed that Turkey and Greece formed an indispensable barrier to Soviet moves around Europe's southern flank into the Mediterranean. Once Congress had accepted the principle of Truman's containment policy, it became easier to subsume the mounting sums for Greek and Turkish aid under the general European rubric than to fight separate annual battles of appropriations. One result thus has been that Turkey in the past four decades has become one of the steadiest recipients of U.S. military and economic aid —its grand total exceeded only by Britain and France, South Korea and South Vietnam, and, most recently, Egypt and Israel.

Minor divergences, nonetheless, developed over the Middle East. İnönü's government was eager to keep its distance from Islamic neighbors and to emphasize the Western, secular character of Ankara's policy; thus Turkey in 1949 became the first Middle Eastern country to establish relations with Israel.[11] American policymakers, on the contrary, wished to take advantage of the new ally's commitment to collective defense by integrating Turkey both into their European strategy and into their more tentative plans for the Balkans and the Middle East. Eager to confirm Tito's break with Moscow, Washington encouraged Turkey and Greece to conclude pacts of collaboration and military assistance with Yugoslavia (1953–54). In 1951, London and Washington invited Turkey and Egypt to join in forming a "Middle East Command," which, it was hoped, would preserve the Western military position on the Suez Canal. In 1954, Turkey itself sought to implement Washington's conception of a defense of the Middle East's "Northern Tier" by concluding a mutual assistance agreement with Pakistan, subsequently enlarged into the Baghdad Pact and including Iran, Iraq, and Great Britain.

All these Middle Eastern defense schemes proved ill conceived. Egypt itself repudiated the Middle East Command and, after Nasser's coup of 1952, moved toward neutralism and alignment with Moscow. The Baghdad Pact hastened the upheaval which, by 1958, turned Iraq into one of Moscow's closest friends in the Middle East. Although the pact itself, grandiosely renamed the Central Treaty Organization, lingered on for two more decades, it amounted to little more than parallel U.S. aid programs for Turkey, Iran, and Pakistan.

Ankara clearly had been right in the 1940s in placing more trust in Washington's plans for Europe. Yet the Menderes government in the 1950s joined those futile diplomatic exercises in the Middle East less from strategic conviction than from a growing appetite for U.S. aid to cover the mounting deficits of rapid and uneven economic development.

As these examples indicate, the close harmony and full success of the joint Turkish-American containment policy over the years implied certain dangers. As the acute Soviet threat receded, the attention of each ally naturally enough turned elsewhere: Washington's to distant locations such as Vietnam—and the resulting foreign policy malaise of the American public; Ankara's to problems of foreign debt and international payments or the fate of fellow nationals on Cyprus. Just because the alliance was so solidly established, each side now was tempted to take the relationship for granted or to use the other as a means to extraneous ends: Ankara to cover its financial deficits, and Washington in pursuit of its "pactomania" or global strategy. Thus President Kennedy did not take time to consult Ankara on the decision to remove American Jupiter missiles from Turkey in the wake of the Cuban missile crisis of 1962. Understandably, Ankara was annoyed.

Another temporary irritant in Turkish-American relations in the 1960s was the poppy question. Turkey had long been one of the major cultivators of poppies; and the Ankara government over the years had joined the relevant international agreements controlling the legal trade in opium for pharmaceutical purposes. Although there is no widespread narcotics addiction in Turkey itself, Washington officials by the 1960s identified Turkey as one of the major sources of illegal heroin supplies reaching the United States. After various attempts to control or limit poppy growing, a 1971 agreement provided for the complete elimination of poppy cultivation by 1972, in return for $35 million in temporary U.S. financial assistance to compensate the Anatolian cultivators and help them shift to other crops. The program would appear to have been a full success—although it evidently had no effect on the total volume of global heroin trade, including such regions as Latin America and Southern Asia.

The Cyprus Stumbling Block

As it turned out, the biggest shadow over U.S.-Turkish relations came to be cast not by any developments in the the Middle East or disagreements over missiles or opium, but rather by the Cyprus question. The dispute itself was a legacy of the way in which Great Britain effected that particular phase of its imperial withdrawal. Occupied by Britain in 1878, Cyprus had become a crown colony in 1914. In contrast to British "protectorates" or "mandates" such as Egypt, Iraq, or Transjordan, Cyprus had no indigenous government to which London might transfer political responsibility. Nor, of course, had Cyprus been included in the Greek-Turkish population exchange after 1923, which settled most outstanding issues between those two countries. Indeed, British administrators on Cyprus had found it convenient to divide and rule—that is, to preserve or emphasize rather than merge the cultural differences between Greeks and Turks.

In the event, the Cyprus issue was brought to a head in the 1950s by the Greek-Cypriot guerrilla movement of General George Grivas, whose declared aim for Cyprus was enosis, or union with Greece. Conscious of the precarious position of the island's 18 percent Turkish minority, Turkey first emphasized that it had no complaint about continuing British rule (just as, two decades earlier, Ankara had not raised the question of the ethnic Turkish minority in Alexandrette until France had announced its intention to terminate its mandate over Syria). When, regardless of Ankara's protestations, Britain invited

Turkish and Greek representatives to confer about Cyprus and its impending decolonization, Turkey took an increasingly nationalistic, intransigent line. Greek atrocities against Cypriot Turks became a staple of the Istanbul mass-circulation daily *Hürriyet*; and Prime Minister Menderes, finding irredentism a convenient diversion from economic troubles at home, supported semiofficially a Cyprus-Is-Turkish Association with the slogan "Partition or Death."

By 1959, the British-Greek-Turkish negotiations in Zurich and London had resulted in an agreement that declared Cyprus independent without partition as of February 1960. The island was to have a legislature with separate representation for the Greek and Turkish communities; an elected Greek-Cypriot president and Turkish-Cypriot vice president; a mutual veto on major policy issues; two extraterritorial British bases in the south; and a Treaty of Guarantee authorizing Britain, Greece, and Turkey to station troops on the island and to intervene, jointly or separately, if the constitutional status quo was violated.

Alas, the delicate arrangement devised over the course of years and laid down in the Zurich-London accords broke down within a few months—unimplemented. The flag adopted for Cyprus as a "new nation" symbolized the basic difficulty: blue, red, or green were out as the colors of Greece, Turkey, and Islam, respectively; crescents, stars, crosses, or stripes were unacceptable for similar reasons. At last the resourceful designers came up with a map of the island in yellow on white; yet with the Greek and the Turkish flags accorded equal status, few Cypriots ever made use of the pale contrivance. Only His Beatitude Archbishop Makarios, whom his fellow Greek-Cypriots elected president, gave some plausibility to Cyprus as an independent nation. Finding the prospect of enosis under shifting governments in Athens incompatible with his own ambitions, he developed instead a potent appeal to Third World and anticolonialist sentiment in the UN General Assembly.

Makarios and his Greek-Cypriot followers soon set aside the unworkable constitution, and communal friction increased, with members of the Turkish minority being forced to flee from

many parts of the island and suffering heavy casualties. Early
in 1964, Under Secretary of State George W. Ball, sent by Washington to mediate the dispute, warned Makarios that "the
world's not going to stand idly by and let you turn this beautiful
little island into your private abattoir."[12] When the mediation
effort failed, Turkey informed Washington by midyear that it
intended to use its right of intervention under the 1960 Treaty
of Guarantee. This time, President Johnson, preoccupied with
Vietnam and eager to avoid further diplomatic crises, sent a
letter to Prime Minister İsmet İnönü, warning against the use of
American-made equipment in any expedition to Cyprus; if
Turkish action provoked "Soviet intervention," Washington
would have to reconsider whether its NATO "obligation to
protect Turkey" would apply.[13]

If Ball's indelicacy had antagonized Makarios, Johnson's
even greater bluntness profoundly shocked Turkey; and neither move brought the crisis closer to resolution. In view of
Johnson's threatening message, Ankara reluctantly called off
the invasion at the last moment. In Washington, Johnson's
letter had remained a secret among five or six top officials; in
Ankara, Prime Minister İsmet İnönü was obliged to share it
with his cabinet; and when the text leaked to the Turkish press,
the damage to U.S.-Turkish relations was severe. Only a decade earlier, Turkey had eagerly dispatched its troops to help the
United States fight communist aggression in Korea; now Johnson's letter amounted to threatening America's Turkish ally
with the common Soviet enemy. The feeling of betrayal in Turkey was widespread.

A decade later, on July 15, 1974, the Greek military forces on
Cyprus, on orders from the ruling junta in Athens, engineered
a coup under the right-wing extremist Nikos Sampson that
would have forced enosis and dispensed with any semblance of
democratic freedom even among Greek Cypriots. Archbishop
Makarios himself barely escaped with his life through a back
door of his palace. This time the Ankara government did invoke its treaty right of intervention without awaiting Washington's reaction. On July 20 to 22, 1974, Ankara's military forces
occupied the northern, mainly Turkish-populated, portion of

the island. The result was the collapse of Sampson's coup and, a few days later, of the right-wing junta in Athens that had instigated the desperate scheme. After seven years of military dictatorship, Greece once again had a democratic government.

In dispatching its troops to Cyprus in July 1974, Turkey had responded to the imminent danger to its conationals from Sampson's fascist coup. Ankara could also justifiably claim that the 1960 Cyprus Treaty of Guarantee gave each of the signatories (United Kingdom, Greece, Turkey) the right to intervene, jointly or singly, and by force if necessary, to prevent the destruction of the constitutional order which they had pledged to guarantee.[14]

The Turkish landings, which had helped to thwart right-wing militarist designs both in Nicosia and in Athens, met with much sympathy abroad, and for some weeks intensive mediation efforts between Ankara and the new government in Athens continued. Yet it soon turned out that the overcautious Turkish military had fallen short of their full operational goals; and from August 14 to 17 Turkish forces resumed their advance to occupy a total of 37 percent of the island. This second intervention carried the occupation far beyond the area of solid Turkish settlement; and it came after any acute danger to the Cypriot-Turkish minority had passed and democracy in Greece had been restored. Hence it was this second intervention far more than the first that, immediately and over the years, subjected Ankara to severe criticism in Greece and among its friends in Europe, America, and the Third World.

On Cyprus, Turkey's military intervention of 1974 established two separate de facto regimes: the Greek-Cypriot government under Makarios, and later Spyros Kyprianou; and the Turkish-Cypriot government headed by Rauf Denktash. Although Turkish forces have remained in occupation of the north, calm has returned to the island as a result of the de facto partition; indeed, the prosperous Greek part in the late 1970s and early 1980s substantially benefited from the exodus of many commercial firms from war-torn Lebanon 150 miles to the southeast.

Denktash in 1975 proclaimed a Turkish Federated State of

Cyprus, and in 1983 an Independent Turkish Republic of Northern Cyprus.[15] Much to the disappointment of Denktash and his backers in Ankara, neither move prompted international recognition, not even among most of Turkey's fellow members of the Islamic Conference Organization. And repeatedly over the years Denktash emphasized that the proclamations of statehood and independence were meant not to prevent, but rather to stimulate, a negotiated settlement with the Greek-Cypriot side.

Such negotiations have taken place, on and off, for more than a decade and usually under the auspices of the United Nations—most recently throughout 1984. In contrast to the 1960 attempt at creating a unitary binational regime, these have concentrated on the possibility of a bizonal, federal solution. Yet when UN Secretary General Javier Pérez de Cuéllar invited both heads of government to New York in January 1985 to confirm a carefully balanced plan along those lines, Denktash endorsed the plan in toto—whereas the Greek-Cypriot Kyprianou government saw it only as a step toward further negotiation. A new initiative on Pérez de Cuellar's part early in 1986 appeared to meet with similar reluctance on the Greek-Cypriot and Greek side.

Domestic Complications in Ankara and Washington

When the Cyprus crisis erupted in the summer of 1974, it happened that domestic politics in both the United States and Turkey were in a phase of acute crisis that seriously limited Ankara's room for maneuver, and in Washington all but paralyzed the process of government.

In Turkey, two years of martial law and nonpartisan governments (1971–73) had stemmed an intense wave of left- and right-wing terrorism; but the elections of October 1973 that were to restore full democracy had resulted in an unprecedented deadlock. The Republican People's Party, with a new democratic-socialist program, had won a mere plurality—with Demirel's right-of-center Justice Party second, Erbakan's Islamic-conservative Salvation Party (with a record 11.8 percent of the popular vote) in the crucial third place, and dissident groups from both major parties dividing most of the remaining seats. As the new parliament assembled, more than three months were consumed in vain attempts to form minority governments under Ecevit or Demirel, or a coalition between them, or yet another bureaucratic caretaker cabinet.

Finally, in February 1974, Ecevit won a narrow parliamentary majority for a government coalition of his RPP with the Salvationists—an outcome perhaps best described as a marriage of inconvenience between secularist social democrats and militant Islamic conservatives. The RPP itself only recently had gone through a wrenching leadership contest in which İsmet İnönü—Atatürk's former front commander in the War of Independence, architect of the 1923 peace treaty, president of his country in the difficult years of World War II, and after 1950 its first opposition leader—had been dethroned at the age of eighty-eight as leader of the RPP by Bülent Ecevit, whose career as party secretary the "old fox" had long overshadowed.

During the eight months of Ecevit's and Erbakan's incongruous coalition, a firm nationalist stand on Cyprus provided one of the few policies on which both sides could readily agree. Ecevit personally took some pride in that he, unlike the octogenarian ex-general a decade earlier, would not be bullied by Washington into canceling the Cyprus landing. He took equal pride in his personal relationship with Henry Kissinger, whose seminars he had attended while a postgraduate fellow at Harvard, and who, at the height of the crisis, was on the phone with him several times a day.

Turkey's critics in Washington were not concerned with those partisan complications in Ankara; nor were they particularly concerned with the 1960 Treaty of Guarantee, which Turkey invoked to justify its intervention but to which the United States was not a party. Rather, they pointed to a 1947 U.S.-Turkish agreement and to applicable U.S. laws which limited Turkey's use of American military equipment to self-defense, collective action under the UN charter, or other purposes specifically approved by the United States.

The feeling was widespread in Washington (as Henry Kissinger put it in retrospect) that "there was nothing we needed less than a crisis—especially one that would involve two NATO allies."[16] But in Congress, there was no inclination to give the Nixon administration carte blanche in forestalling such a crisis. For whereas Ankara had recently overcome its parliamentary deadlock, Washington happened to be in the midst of a full-scale confrontation between the White House and Congress.

In the three-and-a-half weeks between the first and second Turkish landings on Cyprus, the House had voted to impeach the President, Nixon had found it advisable to resign, and Gerald Ford had succeeded at the White House. While the Watergate burglary of 1972 had prompted the constitutional confrontation, secrecy in foreign policy with regard to Cambodia had provided an additional count in the indictment against Nixon.

In this atmosphere of tension and antagonism, exchanges with regard to Cyprus between Secretary Kissinger and members of Congress quickly turned into a contest over executive privilege versus legislative supremacy. When Kissinger at one point faulted a Democratic senator for not understanding the foreign policy priorities, the tart reply was, "Mr. Secretary, you do not understand the rule of law." On the House floor, a member urged adoption of the anti-Turkish embargo so that the State Department "would not thumb its nose at the Congress [and] the law of the land." By October 1974, Congress proceeded to enact legislation which suspended all military assistance and sales to Turkey.

Compared to this atmosphere of constitutional crisis and Kissinger's unwillingness to tolerate what he saw as congressional interference in foreign policy, the much-discussed attempts by Greek-American organizations to influence the decision to impose an embargo appear to have played a reinforcing rather than an initiating role. Indeed, once the Watergate atmosphere receded and better relations were established between Congress and the State Department, there began a concerted effort to limit the damage.

Specifically, the congressional leadership agreed with the

White House to postpone the effective date of the embargo from December 1974 to February 1975 so as to provide an opportunity for negotiation. Unfortunately, Turkey was in no position to take advantage of the delay; for in September Premier Ecevit had broken up his incongruous Republican-Salvationist coalition in hopes of forcing an election and, riding the popularity of his Cyprus policy, of securing an absolute majority for his own left-of-center party. The only flaw in this calculation was that the smaller parties feared just such an outcome, so that the call for new elections stood no chance of obtaining the necessary parliamentary approval. Instead, Turkey once again strung along with caretaker governments for six-and-a-half months—until March 1975 when Süleyman Demirel of the Justice Party managed to piece together a coalition including the Muslim-conservative Salvationists and the ultraright Nationalist Action Party. In June 1975 the new Ankara government responded to the congressional embargo on U.S. military aid by announcing the suspension of American (as distinct from NATO) base facilities in Turkey.

Strains in the Alliance

The impasse over Cyprus caused much resentment in both Greece and Turkey and gave rise to a number of new and protracted disputes. The Athens government from 1974 to 1980 withdrew from active military participation in NATO. It also proclaimed an extension of its territorial waters around Greece's islands from six to ten miles—which, if accepted, would close off Turkish passage from the Straits and its Aegean harbors to the Mediterranean—and protested Turkey's search for oil under the disputed waters. There has been a further prolonged dispute as to which country should control air traffic over the Aegean. And in 1982, Greece—against the explicit provisions of the 1923 Treaty of Lausanne and over sharp Turkish protests—remilitarized the island of Lemnos at the western end of the Turkish Straits.

For Turkey, by far the worst consequence of the unresolved Cyprus dispute has been the recurrent friction in relations with the United States, notably the congressionally imposed embargo, from 1975 through 1978, on American military aid and weapons sales to Turkey. The pressure from Congress, however, did not have the intended effect of making Ankara withdraw its troops from the island. Indeed, as Henry Kissinger complained, "the heavy-handed arms embargo against Turkey. . .destroyed all possibility of American mediation" over Cyprus.[17] And as time passed, even pro-embargo congressmen appreciated that such a measure could be "effective as a threat, but once imposed, lost its effectiveness as leverage."[18] As we noted, Ankara, far from knuckling under, retaliated by the measured step of closing a number of U.S. military installations in Turkey.

In relations between Ankara and Athens, there had been occasional direct meetings between Prime Minister Constantine Karamanlis and Premiers Ecevit and Demirel. Yet in view of the unresolved Cyprus issue and the multiplying bilateral problems in the Aegean, the situation of NATO's southern flank remained precarious. The shrill anti-American and often pro-Soviet rhetoric of Greek Premier Andreas Papandreou since 1981 was bound to add to the existing friction.

A further difficulty for Turkey's foreign relations has been the two-pronged revanchist attack by certain Armenian organizations. One of these has been an outright campaign of assassination and terrorism, which since 1973 has claimed the lives of thirty Turkish diplomats, mostly in Western Europe and North America. This, in turn, has necessitated a set of elaborate precautions that has vastly complicated the daily conduct of Turkey's diplomacy. Only twice did this terrorist campaign manage to penetrate Turkey itself, claiming nine lives at Ankara airport in 1982, and three in the Istanbul grand bazaar in 1983. The main organization responsible for these attacks is the Armenian Secret Army for the Liberation of Armenia (ASALA), known to enjoy both Soviet and Syrian support, but disavowed by the Armenian World Congress in Lausanne in 1983.

A more broadly supported undertaking, particularly among Americans of Armenian background, has been the endeavor to equate the widespread killings of Armenians in the late Ottoman period with the Nazi Holocaust of European Jewry, and somehow to associate the present-day Turkish Republic with those events of seventy or ninety years ago. The argument is weak for a number of reasons.

First, it was the historically unique *millet* system of religious autonomy which assured the communal survival of Armenians, Greeks, Sephardic Jews, and other ethnic-religious groups under many centuries of Ottoman-Turkish rule. This historic Ottoman pattern of institutionalized tolerance stood in sharpest contrast to the experience of Europe from the Middle Ages to the seventeenth century: of expulsion or forced conversion of Muslims and Jews; of systematic persecution of Christian "heretics"; and of intolerance or religious wars among Orthodox Christians, Catholics, and Protestants.

Second, for the Ottoman Turks, the peaceful coexistence of religious groups had been a source of strength and of pride as they extended their empire through the Middle East and North Africa and deep into Europe. But that same multinational and multireligious pattern turned into a major liability in the Ottomans' final period of retreat and decline.

For a century (1804–1918) European imperialist pressure from outside and secessionist uprisings from inside combined to bring national independence to Serbia, Greece, Romania, Bulgaria, and Albania; and imposed a change from Ottoman to European rulers on most Arab countries. In response, the Ottoman rulers, not unlike the Tsarist officials of the same period, were torn between introducing broad civic reforms for subjects of all faiths and nationalities—or condoning the vengeful instincts of the (Russian-Orthodox, Turkish-Muslim) majority. Greeks dominated the Ottoman foreign service of the early nineteenth century; Christians and Jews actively participated in the political parties and elections of the constitutional period after 1908; and the grand vezir under whose leadership the Ottoman government entered World War I was an Egyptian of Albanian descent. At other times there were major ethnic massacres, against Greeks in 1832, Bulgarians in 1878, and Armenians in 1896 and 1915. Those events would seem closely analogous to the Russian pogroms of the same period. In both situations the attempt to reorganize a multinational empire into territorial nation-states caused mounting friction, with the heaviest, unforgivable cost in human lives paid by the numerically smaller and geographically scattered minorities such as the Jews of the Pale and the Armenians of Anatolia.

Third, Hitler's demand for the extermination of the Jews for the salvation of the German "master race" has no equivalent in any of the political ideologies of the Ottoman Empire—let alone in Atatürk's nation-state with its commitment to "Peace at home, peace in the world." Indeed, Atatürk himself in 1926 publicly stated that some of the late Ottoman politicians "should have been made to account" for the killing of "millions of our Christian subjects" during World War I.[19]

To remove the Armenian question as an irritant in relations between Washington and Ankara, what is needed most is a broader perspective. Turkey's leaders—and in particular the more sensationalist segments of the country's press—would do well to realize that not every nonbinding resolution passed by Congress constitutes a major pronouncement of U.S. policy. Perhaps the Ankara government, which in the midst of the ongoing Cyprus controversy in the mid-1980s found it possible to open its frontiers to Greek visitors without the traditional visa requirement, might find it possible to reemphasize Atatürk's just-quoted repudiation of the Ottoman mass killings of Armenians during World War I. In Washington, congressmen would do well to appreciate that to dwell on a one-sided picture of the past will not help improve present or future relations with our key Atlantic-Middle Eastern ally and, indeed, that Armenian terrorism is one of the prime means by which Moscow and Damascus have hoped to drive a wedge between Turkey and the West.

Reaching Out and Rebuilding

U.S.-Turkish relations were strained in the wake of the 1974 invasion of Cyprus and the subsequent congressional embargo. Remarkably, however, Turkish opinion did not—as might well have been expected in other countries—take any

decisive turn to neutralism or anti-Americanism. The closing of
U.S. (rather than NATO) bases in Turkey restored something
of a bilateral negotiating position; and soon, both Washington
and Ankara were careful to limit the damage of the embargo.
By October 1975, Congress itself acted to exempt from the embargo military deliveries contracted for before the effective date
of the embargo, and in fact the military deliveries for 1975 and
1976 were not substantially lower than for the previous year.
Above all, through the active commitment of the Ford and
Carter administrations in Washington and successive governments in Ankara, American-Turkish military cooperation was
maintained within the convenient and extensive framework of
the Atlantic alliance.

Furthermore, during the period of maximum strain in Washington's relationship with Turkey, Ankara had responded con-
structively by giving its diplomacy a broader outreach.
Turkey's continuing status as a full member of NATO (since
1952) and an associate member of the European Community
(since 1964), its more recent association with the Islamic Conference Organization (1976),[20] the détente in its relations with the
Soviet Union, and its thriving trade with the Middle East and
scrupulous neutrality in the Iraq-Iran war since 1980 may all be
seen as important elements in this trend of diversification.

By April 1978, President Carter personally committed himself to the lifting of the Turkish embargo. In September Congress finally agreed, and in Febuary 1979 arms shipments were
resumed. By January 1979, Under Secretary of State Warren B.
Christopher was off to Ankara to negotiate what was to become, a year later, the U.S.-Turkish Defense and Economic
Cooperation Agreement (DECA) of 1980; and later that year,
Bernard Rogers, the U.S. general in command of NATO, in
intense and confidential negotiations with Athens and Ankara,
secured Greece's full reentry into the alliance.

If Ecevit and other leftists had toyed with the idea of neutralism in the late 1970s, the Soviet invasion of Afghanistan in
December 1979 did much to reconfirm their strategic commitment to the West. On the Turkish side, the 1980 DECA was
negotiated by successive governments under Ecevit and De-

mirel, to be implemented by General Evren's junta and Turgut Özal's civilian government—demonstrating once again the nonpartisan character of Turkey's foreign policy and of its commitment to the special relationship with the United States.

Six

Turkey, the Middle East, and the West: Problems and Opportunities

Turkey and America's Global Policies

In March 1986, Secretary of State George Shultz traveled to Turkey on a trip that included an extended visit to the Istanbul bazaar and further conversations on the renewal of the 1980 Defense and Economic Cooperation Agreement. This agreement, which regulates the use of American military bases, military assistance, and other matters of common security interest, had been extended, upon its expiry in December 1985, on an annual basis so as to allow for broader negotiations. At one of the scheduled social events, the Secretary found himself faced with insistent Turkish demands that the new DECA be linked to a substantial increase in the quota for Turkish textile imports to the United States. "I have been brought here in order to have a nice luncheon and instead get hit behind the ear," he complained to an accompanying journalist.[1]

The small contretemps in American-Turkish diplomacy emphasizes the need for better mutual understanding and broader contacts now that Turkey's economic transformation has progressed to the point where Ankara is as eager for American trade as for American aid.

Secretary Shultz's visit came nearly forty years after the ceremonial visit of the U.S.S. *Missouri* to Istanbul's harbor in April 1946 first demonstrated the American commitment under what was to become the Truman Doctrine. Our intensive relations with Turkey began after the end of World War II, as Washing-

106

ton was shaping its distinctive policies toward three major world regions: the industrial nations of Western Europe, the British Commonwealth, and Japan; the Soviet Union and other communist countries; and the developing countries of what soon became known as the "Third World." Turkey, situated in both Europe and Asia and directly on the Soviet border, turned out to be of special relevance to each of those three strands in our global policy.

Against the threat from the communist "Second World," Ankara had formulated its own policy of containment nearly two years before Washington's Truman Doctrine. Having opted for Western culture in Atatürk's day, Turkey also showed its eagerness for acceptance to the West, or "First World," by launching its transition to democracy and joining in collective self-defense as far away as South Korea and the North Atlantic. Democratization, in turn, sped Turkey's economic growth as a developing "Third World" nation. In the decades since the Truman Doctrine, each strand of Washington's long-range global policy thus found a stronger resonance and more purposeful field of application in Turkey than in most other locales.

The success of anti-Soviet containment in Turkey has been striking. The border near Kars and on Mount Ararat not only became the first arena in the incipient Cold War—but remains the only direction where communist power has never expanded beyond the original 1921 frontiers of the Soviet Union. Turkey's place in the West's collective security is unique in that it furnishes electronic stations along the Black Sea coast that are closest to Soviet missile launching and atomic testing sites in Central Asia. Turkey thus constitutes the powerful southern flank in NATO's anti-Soviet defenses; and its function as a barrier to Soviet penetration of the Middle East has become even more crucial since the fall of the Shah in Iran.

Another major policy strand, antedating the Truman Doctrine, was American aid in the postwar reconstruction of Europe and Japan—soon broadened into support for economic and political integration in Europe through the Marshall Plan and the Common Market; and for financial and economic coordination throughout the "First World" through institutions such as the IMF and the OECD. Turkey, not having been part of the European theater of war, did not become a focal point for those postwar endeavors; yet its "First World" associations continued apace. As an early recipient of Marshall Plan aid, Turkey joined the OECD and the Council of Europe. In due course, it became an associate member of the European Economic Community (to which, as we saw, nearly two million Turkish citizens have migrated in search of employment), and it now intends to apply for full membership. In the 1980s Turkey became one of the debtor countries that successfully applied the formulas for economic restructuring and recovery offered by the IMF and the World Bank.

Washington's economic and technical assistance to underdeveloped countries, embodied in programs such as Truman's "Point Four" and Kennedy's "Alliance for Progress," proved somewhat inconsistent. The early hopes that foreign aid would quickly secure industrial development and democracy in the postcolonial world turned out to be overoptimistic; and soon such longer-range goals yielded to more immediate geopolitical and strategic considerations as the Cold War scene shifted to East Asia, the Middle East, and Central America.

In this varied Third World context, Turkey remains one nation where strategic, economic, and political considerations have fully converged. In Turkey, as in Taiwan and South Korea, American aid did contribute to rapid industrialization. Turkey is also one of the exceptional nations where U.S.-supported educational and economic development since the 1950s became a key factor in promoting the indigenous growth of democratic attitudes and institutions. And while Turkey has suffered notable setbacks on the road both to industrialization and democracy, the increasing momentum in both directions has carried it far ahead of the typical Third World country.

The United States, Turkey, and the Middle East

Although Washington's policy analysts tend to class Turkey, along with Spain and Portugal, as NATO's southern flank, its central importance remains that of a strategic link between Europe and the turbulent Middle East. In that latter region, the years of the congressional embargo on military aid to Turkey and its lifting (1975–79) coincided with an extensive transformation, including the Camp David peace talks between Egypt and Israel (1978), the Iranian Revolution and hostage crisis (1978–79), and the Soviet invasion of Afghanistan (1979). The early 1980s continued that hectic pace: the Iraq-Iran war (since 1980); President Reagan's proposal to solve the Palestinian problem in association with Jordan (1982) and the subsequent failure of preliminary negotiations between King Hussein and the PLO (1986); Israel's invasion of Lebanon and the dispatch of U.S. Marines to Beirut (1982–84); the second explosion of OPEC's oil price (1979–81) and its near-collapse (1986); and the Reagan administration's confrontation with Libya (1986).

In contrast to this kaleidoscopic Middle Eastern scene, the Defense and Economic Cooperation Agreement of 1980 has restored Turkish-American ties to normalcy. Over the past forty years, Ankara's alliance with Washington has added an essential link to the West's defense and posed a major obstacle to the furthering of Moscow's interests in the Middle East.

The Soviet Union over the years formed close ties with one or another Arab country—first, in the wake of Britain's withdrawal, with Nasser's Egypt in 1955 and Iraq in 1958; more recently with the PLO, Syria, Libya, and South Yemen. Nonetheless, the dramatic shift from Nasser's pro-Soviet to Sadat's pro-Western course, as well as Moscow's changing relations with Baghdad, suggests how fragile such ties can be. The bloody showdown in Lebanon in 1983 between Syrian and PLO forces, each armed with Soviet weapons, starkly demonstrates Moscow's difficulty in controlling its presumed "proxies" at a distance. By the mid-1980s there were signs that Moscow was eager to demonstrate its reasonableness in wishing to be included in any future Arab-Israeli peace negotiations.

It is Turkey's firm alliance with the West that makes possible Moscow's recurrent setbacks in Cairo, Baghdad, and other Arab capitals. Only behind Turkey's protective shield can governments in Egypt, Iraq, or Syria afford to lean now toward

Moscow and now toward Washington without courting the fate of Czechoslovakia, Hungary, or Afghanistan. Only behind that same Turkish barrier can Israel maintain its status as a regional power and cope with continuing Arab hostility without the risk of facing on the Golan Heights not just Soviet arms supplied to Syria but the full force of the Red Army itself.

Turkey's presence as a Western ally wedged between Soviet Russia and the Arab countries thus is crucial for preserving stability in the Middle East and, in a broad sense, neutralizing the region as an arena in the East-West conflict. Specifically, the Turkish barrier gives fullest scope to two inherent tendencies in the region—toward what might be termed checkerboard divisions and self-adjusting realignments.

Almost every country in the Middle East is at odds with its neighbors and hence eager to be in league with its neighbors once removed. For all the intense rhetoric about Arab unity since the 1950s, the only unification scheme that briefly worked was the United Arab Republic (1958–61) between Egypt and Syria—which were not immediate neighbors but joined in common hostility against Israel. Since the geographic map does not neatly line up in squares, the checkerboard pattern remains imperfect, and prompts a number of dramatic switches. Notably, when conflict does erupt, as in the Iraq-Iran war since 1980, the tendency of nearby states is to shift to the support of the weaker side—hence the rallying of the Gulf Cooperation Council, Jordan, and Egypt to Iraq after 1982.

Similarly, in relations with outside powers, the inveterate Middle Eastern practice is to play off the faraway foreigner against the foreigner nearby. This is why Turkey, on Russia's frontier for the last four centuries, has been our closest ally in the Middle East; and why even Iran, after its convulsive revolution, turned not only anti-Western but also anti-Soviet. Syria's alignment with Moscow fits in well with the checkerboard pattern, for it borders on both Israel and Turkey, our own closest allies. Elsewhere in the core of the Middle East and at a safe distance from the Soviets, countries such as Egypt and Iraq have leaned now toward the Soviets, now toward the West, or back toward neutralism, depending on their changing assessment of the current and prospective regional balance—the most dramatic switch, of course, being that by Egypt's Sadat in the early 1970s. And it is at the remote, southern end of the region, in South Yemen and Ethiopia, that the Soviets have registered their most solid successes.

By contrast, the United States, two oceans away and without colonialist designs in the region, is not generally considered an acute threat. The Soviet Union is respected for its military strength, as a supplier of weapons, and a counterweight to the West. By contrast, American goods—from nylon stockings and bluejeans to reruns of Hollywood movies—have long set the standards for affluent consumers, and American college degrees are valued by the upwardly mobile. That the United States can be freely criticized by both Americans and their friends and enemies constitutes, on balance, an added attraction.

Together, the checkerboard and realignment syndromes account for the remarkable fact that, despite the enormous flow of weapons into the Middle East since the 1950s, its political boundaries have not significantly changed since the partition of the Ottoman Empire after World War I.[2]

In sum, the Middle East's central location at the juncture of three continents and two oceans—between Europe, the Soviet Union, and the Third World—implies enormous potential risks for world peace and hence for U.S. global strategy. Yet those risks are largely neutralized by the Turkish barrier and those regional tendencies toward balance of power.

It was the joint desire to establish that barrier that first prompted Turkish-American cooperation: Ankara's determination to fight Soviet territorial demands "to the last Turk," and President Truman's support of "free peoples resisting attempted subjugation. . .by outside pressure." Those same considerations retain their validity in the late twentieth century: Turkey would be directly threatened by any Soviet thrust into the Middle East—say, in a political vacuum created in post-Khomeini Iran.

In the region to the south of Turkey, America's policy has

done best when it has reinforced, rather than counteracted, those tendencies toward Middle Eastern balance that we just noted. It could be argued, for example, that our occasional interventions into the domestic politics of Middle Eastern countries have regularly miscarried. At times the failure was immediate and obvious, as in the fiasco of Carter's hostage rescue attempt in Iran (1980) or of Reagan's dispatch of Marines into the midst of a Lebanese civil war (1982–84). At other times the mistake was arguable at least in retrospect, as with our encouragement of the Greek colonels' coup of 1967—which largely accounts for the recent popularity of Prime Minister Andreas Papandreou's anti-American rhetoric; or the CIA's role in restoring the Shah to power in 1953—which provided twenty-five years of apparent stability at the cost of undermining the Shah's popularity and redoubling the anti-American fury of Iran's revolution.

By contrast, Washington's Mideast policy registered notable successes when mediating between parties willing to make peace—as at Camp David; or in responding to the requests of friendly countries for protection from aggressive neighbors—as in the dispatch of AWACS planes in 1984 to avert Libya's threat to Egypt, and to counter Iran's threat to Saudi oil ports. Similarly, we have done well in reinforcing the regional checkerboard and realignment patterns—notably by supporting Sadat's break with Moscow, and reestablishing diplomatic relations with Iraq in 1984 at a time when the Iranian counteroffensives assumed menacing proportions.

Our most successful stance in the Middle East has been to encourage a pattern of peaceful pluralism—an attitude of live and let live. Such a tolerant policy toward the Middle East accords well with the inherent pluralist tendencies of American society, which has connected with the Middle East by sending missionaries, educators, military and economic aid, and Zionist funds; and by attracting Greek and Armenian immigrants, Arab petrodollars, and students from all parts of the region. That same emphasis on tolerance and balance, moreover, is all but imperative for the United States, which in a few decades has emerged as the paramount outside power in the Middle East without ever establishing any colonies in the region.

Since the late 1940s, our friends in the Middle East have included Israel, a vibrant immigrant democracy; Turkey, a developing democracy with interludes of military rule; one-party regimes as in Sadat's Egypt or Bourguiba's Tunisia; constitutional monarchies as in Morocco and Jordan; traditional monarchies as in Saudi Arabia and the Gulf sheikdoms; and military regimes such as Pakistan. Our closest and most durable relations among these have continued under changing regimes: with Israel under Labor, Likud, and national coalition; with Egypt under Sadat and Mubarak; and in Turkey, where, as we noted, the DECA of 1980 was negotiated under shifting parliamentary coalitions, and implemented by the Evren junta and, after 1983, by Özal's democratic government.

What has evolved between Washington and Ankara over the decades is a basic strategic consensus within NATO and on containment of the Soviet Union—and occasional divergences on policy in the Eastern Mediterranean or Middle East. In the 1950s, Ankara was glad to support U.S. regional initiatives, such as the Middle East Command or the Balkan and "Northern Tier" pacts; yet most of these, as we noted in Chapter 5, proved stillborn. With Turkey's entry into NATO, electronic installations along the Black Sea coast proved their value as listening posts closest to Soviet test sites; and the American U-2 reconnaissance plane downed by the Soviets in 1960 had taken off from an airfield in southern Turkey. In the late 1970s, despite the congressional arms embargo on Turkey, close military cooperation continued in the NATO framework.

Of course, with Turkey as with our other Atlantic allies, military moves outside the NATO region have to be concerted on a case-by-case basis. Thus Turkey in 1957 successfully counteracted a concentration of Soviet arms on its Syrian frontier with a partial mobilization of its own; and Turkish airfields were available for our landing in Lebanon in 1958. By contrast, Turkey did not cooperate with our aerial resupply of weapons to Israel in 1973, or later with the ill-fated hostage-rescue mission to Iran (1980) or the equally ill-fated mission to Beirut (1982–84).

Meanwhile, the upgrading of airfields in eastern Turkey in the early 1980s makes the country more valuable not only as a part of NATO's southern flank, but also as a possible base for "rapid deployment" in the Middle East. Turkey is unlikely to permit the use of those airfields for one-sided regional interventions, say in an Israeli-Arab conflict. Yet there is no question that we will be able to count on Turkey's full cooperation to protect the Middle East against Soviet attack—notably to help prevent a military push across Iran toward Iraq or the Gulf.

Probably our relations will never be as close with Turkey as they are with Israel. Both the United States and Israel are societies founded by pioneers upon an ideal vision of the future; and both continue to draw strength from the absorption of immigrants of the most diverse backgrounds. America's Jewish population, larger than Israel's and active on the American cultural and political scene, provides an even more direct link. Yet it would be unrealistic to conclude, as did Secretary of State Alexander Haig in 1981–82, that Israel should be our chief "strategic ally" in the Middle East and thus provide the basis for a "regional consensus."

Israel, regardless of specific prospects for a resolution of the Palestine question, is likely to remain in recurrent tension with some of its Arab neighbors. Above all, Israel is too far from the Soviet border to serve as a protective umbrella. It is Turkey to which geography assigns that role—and which therefore keeps Israel as well as the Arab countries from facing the Soviets as an overwhelming military threat. In contrast to Israel, Turkey is on good terms with most Middle Eastern countries. Even in the deadlock over Cyprus, and hence in relations with Greece, there are recent indications of potential progress. The one neighbor of whom Turkey has rightly been wary has been the Soviet Union—and even here, relations have moved toward normalcy through mutual strength and respect. If current economic trends continue, Turkey also may become, on a larger scale, the kind of free enterprise and banking oasis in the Middle East desert that Lebanon used to be.

Turkey's friends might hope that Ankara would extend its recent pattern of outreach so as to develop closer relations with Israel. This, indeed could build on the precedent of friendly relations when Turkey recognized the new state of Israel as early as March 1949 and established diplomatic relations in 1950—and when, soon thereafter, Jewish immigrants from Turkey donated a grove of saplings along the road from Tel Aviv to Haifa, complete with an inscription in Turkish and Hebrew dedicating it as the "Atatürk Forest."

Turkey and Israel are America's closest partners in the Middle East; and among their Middle Eastern neighbors, each has the most persistent difficulty with Syria's Soviet-backed policies. Of course, Ankara's downgrading of its Israeli relations after 1967 was in part intended to improve relations with oil-rich Arab countries. But the experience of the United States and Western European countries shows that a balanced foreign policy can include relations with Israelis as well as Arabs. And indeed, in the early 1980s, Israeli and Turkish experts began an unpublicized exchange of information in their common fight against terrorism—specifically on training activities in Lebanon linking the PLO with Armenian, Kurdish, and Turkish terrorist organizations.[3] By the summer of 1986, Turkey and Israel, with equally little publicity, began to upgrade their diplomatic relations.

Political Tensions and Resolutions

American relations with Turkey have evolved in a dynamic environment. Half a century ago, most countries of the Middle East were in Europe's imperial sphere but retained their traditional and patriarchal culture, with political decisions made by kings, shahs, emirs, and a small circle of their (Western or local) advisers. Soon Turkey came to offer an alternate model of political development, with its hard-won national independence and established governmental tradition, its modernizing one-party dictatorship of the 1920s and 1930s, and since the late 1940s, its attempts at an orderly transition to democracy.

The West's imperial departure left the Middle East as a restless congeries of independent states replete with more imported arms, local wars, and savage terrorism than any comparable region. The Arab countries and Iran developed a volatile pattern of political change by assassination, coup, or revolution. Popular ideologies such as Panarabism and Islamic fundamentalism undermined the more traditional allegiances, and demagogues played to xenophobic emotions. The industrial world's dependence on oil and OPEC's price revolution of the 1970s set off a massive inflow of money that increased both the import of arms and social unrest.

Even Turkey, though not subject to the anticolonial backlash or the social upheavals of the oil boom, experienced its own version of unrest from rapid social change. The mass migration of villagers to the city slums—and of high school graduates to the universities in Istanbul and Ankara—gave rise to sporadic outbursts of terrorism; Islamic conservatives and ultranationalists appealed to the fringe electorate; and Marxism developed some substantial appeal among intellectuals and labor leaders. As a result, for a generation, democratic periods have alternated with political paralysis and near-anarchy—and repressive military regimes. By 1983, Turkey emerged from the latest of its military interludes with an uneasy alliance between a military president and a prime minister who is a pious Muslim and advocate of a liberal-capitalist revolution.

What, then, against this restless Middle Eastern background, are the prospects for Turkish politics and for Turkish-American relations? The bombing of Istanbul's chief synagogue during the Jewish sabbath services in September 1986 was a reminder that Turkey is not immune to the kinds of terrorism besetting other Middle Eastern countries.[4] Might Turkey's still somewhat precarious balance between military and democratic politics be upset by future waves of terrorism, by a renewed combination of economic crisis and parliamentary deadlock? Might future Turkish citizens become more susceptible than were their parents to the appeals of Islamic fundamentalism? Does Demirel's reported warning to Evren presage a possibility of military-civilian confrontation after the 1988 legislative and 1989 presidential elections?[5]

There is little question that the Turkish economy will undergo cyclical fluctuations or even occasional full-fledged crises, and that these may cause some sharp reversals at the polls. Yet it is clear that the Turkish political system has steadily broadened and deepened over the years, gaining new strength in overcoming successive setbacks since 1960. The election outcome of 1983, which forced the generals to set a more rapid pace of return to democracy, was itself a triumph of the maturity of the Turkish electorate. The historic tension between secularist and religious attitudes, as we saw, is giving way to a new pattern of tolerance, promoted in part by the recent workers' migration to Europe and closer contacts of Turkey's business elite with the Middle East.

Atatürk had emphasized that his reforms were not directed against religion itself, but intended to separate it from public life. In that basic sense of making religion a matter of private choice, Atatürk's secularist revolution, after half a century, has fully succeeded, at least in the major cities. With the rapid progress of village schools and provincial universities, there is every prospect that the normal and cumulative forces of social change will spread those tolerant religious attitudes, entrenched by now in the urban middle class, throughout society.

In some groups subject to unusual frustrations, there may well be a temporary backlash. Yet as we saw, Turkey's Islamic parties are conservative rather than fundamentalist—and even during the freest and most turbulent democratic periods, they typically polled no more than 5 to 8 percent of the national vote. It is surely significant that Turgut Özal's first attempt at politics, as a provincial candidate for the Islamic-conservative Salvation Party in 1977, ended in defeat and that his second attempt at the head of a democratic and liberal Motherland Party turned into a resounding success. The fact that President Evren, emphatically committed to Atatürk's secularism, has attended and hosted meetings of heads of state of the Islamic Conference Organization is symbolic of an emerging balance and synthesis of Turkey as a secular nation with a majority of Muslim citizens.

The years since 1983 have brought a wider participation and livelier tone to Turkey's political debate than ever before. The initial restrictions on free expression have, in effect, been set aside; yet there has been no reversion to the earlier pattern of deadlock in parliament or terrorism in the streets. The October

1986 synagogue bombing was made possible in part by a lack of security precautions—since there had been no such incidents previously; and throughout 1986 the news from Paris, London, Vienna, Rome, and Athens showed that other European cities were just as susceptible to such terrorist activity.

The institutions of Turkey's Third Republic have helped to focus political debate upon clear alternatives such as Özal's Motherland and Demirel's True Path on the right and İnönü's Social Democrats on the left—with Islamic, ultranationalist, and Marxist groups reduced to virtual insignificance. Even Bülent and Rahşan Ecevit's ideologically oriented Democratic Left finished a poor fourth in the crucial 1986 by-elections—a clear indication that even Turkey's left-wing voters prefer the Social Democrats' moderate and pragmatic approach.

Most observers would expect these democratic trends to continue and indeed to gain further momentum with time. The 1986 by-elections left Özal in control of a legislative majority, but established Demirel as his major challenger on the center-right. There was little question that the political atmosphere of the mid-1980s proved more difficult for a rhetorician and ideologue such as Ecevit than for Demirel, the unsurpassed craftsman of the backroom deal—and the only political leader who (in 1965 and 1969) had gained a popular majority for his party amidst the party fragmentation of the Second Republic. Nonetheless, the 1988 elections are likely to turn into a contest between moderate right and moderate left for the substantial swing vote at the center—and this means that there will be some pressure on the Özal and Demirel camps to compose their differences for fear of throwing the elections to the Social Democrats. The lifting of the political restrictions imposed in 1982–83 would now seem to be irreversible. Indeed one might hope that a lifting of the legal provisions that ban men like Ecevit and Demirel from official political participation would remove the lingering tension. Similarly, the division of labor between the military and political authorities, as embodied in the basic law of 1982 and in understandings between President Evren and Prime Minister Özal, will have to be confirmed or revised under their successors.

Whatever those future details, past experience has confirmed that the military are ready to act as protectors of law and order in the unlikely event of any renewed wave of violence and terror. And the sequel of their interventions, notably in 1961 and 1983, has shown that the military reject any long-term authoritarian solutions, and indeed will bow to the voters' judgment even when it conflicts with their own.

These trends on the electoral and political scene augur well for the future of Turkish foreign policy and of the U.S.-Turkish alliance. Throughout their repeated interventions, the military have retained their respected position in Turkish society; and they have developed a close and time-tested relationship with the United States and NATO military establishments. Similarly, Turkey's foreign service continues its age-old internationalist orientation. Even during the worst period of strain in U.S.-Turkish relations, following the 1974 landings on Cyprus and the congressional embargo, it was Athens that withdrew from military participation in NATO—whereas Ankara balanced its close cooperation within NATO with a new pattern of minidétente with Moscow and outreach toward the Middle East.

Economic Upsurge and Neighborly Relations

Turkey's growing prosperity in the 1980s has, on balance, improved its foreign relations with both Europe and the Middle East. Thus the Özal government in 1985 dispensed with the visa requirement for Greek citizens—and found a steady stream of Greek weekend shoppers headed for the well-stocked stores of border towns such as Edirne. Any basic improvement in relations between Ankara and Athens certainly will have to await the long overdue resolution of the Cyprus question. Here the next move is up to the Greek-Cypriot and Greek sides—since Ankara and Northern Cyprus have accepted in principle the UN proposals of 1985 and 1986 for a bizonal, binational solution.

The Özal government also proclaimed its intention of pressing, at the earliest moment, for Turkey's entry into Europe's

Common Market. Pending the unresolved Cyprus issue, such a move might well run into a veto from Athens. Nonetheless, two previous obstacles to Turkey's integration into the European Economic Community no longer apply. Since 1983 Turkey has gone toward a full restoration of human rights and democratic processes. Indeed, the Council of Europe, which earlier had been among Turkey's most vocal foreign critics, named Ankara's foreign minister Vahit Halefoğlu its presiding officer in July 1986.[6] Meanwhile, Turkey's rapid economic growth in recent years has begun to narrow the wide gap in living standards that has always separated it from Western Europe. Thus, the OECD officially estimated that, for 1986, Turkey was headed for a growth rate of 4.5 percent—highest in that Euro-American-Japanese club of advanced industrial countries.[7]

By contrast to these close and long-standing Western European ties, Turkish relations with Communist Bulgaria went into a phase of sharp tension in the 1980s, prompted first by Ankara's clampdown on the customary drug smuggling and weapons traffic and, by middecade, by Bulgaria's ruthless suppression of its ethnic Turkish minority.

Ankara's relations with Syria, Moscow's closest friend in the Middle East, continued cautious and distant. Syria still has not reconciled itself to the cession of the Hatay border district in 1938. Syria and Syrian-occupied Lebanon, moreover, have long provided the major training centers for Turkish, Kurdish, and Armenian terrorist groups. More recently, Damascus has complained about the giant Atatürk Dam project, which, it fears, will curtail the Euphrates waters Syria now uses further downstream for irrigating its own northeastern plain. To this Ankara responds by assuring Syria that the interruption will be only temporary while the dam fills and asserting its readiness to negotiate details.

Elsewhere in the Middle East, Turkey's newly diversified foreign policy was strikingly illustrated by its close diplomatic relations and lucrative trade with both Iraq and Iran throughout their years of bitter warfare in the 1980s.

Like observers in the United States and some other countries, Turkish economists had mixed feelings about the crumbling of OPEC's cartel structure that, early in 1986, sent the world oil price sliding from $26 to $12 per barrel or less. For Turkey, despite strenuous efforts at substituting domestic coal or hydropower for foreign oil, petroleum remains the largest item on the import bill; hence the price decline presaged an even better balance of payments for the late 1980s. Yet the oil news also fed apprehensions among Turkish contractors and bankers about shutdowns or lagging payments in their once lucrative construction business in the Arab countries.

For the longer run, it was not this or that specific set of projects but Turkey's economic initiative and versatility that would count. In the recent past, Turkey had benefited, at various times, from Western Europe's demand for workers, from the construction boom in Arab oil countries, and from vastly increased trade with Iraq and Iran. In developing those economic relations with the Middle East, the Turks have taken advantage both of their cultural affinity with Islamic neighbors and their own half-century and more of Western educational and technical training—of their "know-who" as well as their "know-how," as some Turkish businessmen on the Middle Eastern circuit are fond of punning.

In the future, Turkey may further stimulate its own economic growth by attracting investments from domestic, Western, and Japanese sources in light industry, agribusines, tourism, and banking. The giant Atatürk Dam, scheduled for completion in the early 1990s, is sure to accelerate agricultural development in Turkey's vast southeastern plain—and incidentally, to create economic opportunities that will help integrate the local Kurdish minorities into the Turkish mainstream. If the protracted Iraq-Iran war should end (perhaps after the Ayatollah Khomeini's death) in a compromise peace, Turkish construction firms are likely to enter yet another contracting boom— this time to rebuild the damaged infrastructure, particularly of Iraq.

Earlier, the shutdown of Beirut as an international banking and trading center created a welcome opportunity for Istanbul to compete for its replacement. In that competition, Istanbul by the mid-1980s was clearly gaining over Athens, with its anti-American governmental rhetoric and persistent airport security problems. The Özal government's campaign to reduce bureaucratic paperwork for foreign trade and investment was slowly bearing fruit. Its broader campaign to dismantle Turkey's overgrown state economic enterprises, dramatically inaugurated by the 1984 bridge bond sale, was not proceeding fast enough to satisfy critics in Turkey's business community. But specific plans were being developed with the advice of experts from the American banking community; and other countries in Europe, Asia, and Latin America experimenting with "privatization" of their own public sectors were looking with keen interest at the Turkish model.

In Turkey itself, the liberal revolution promised by Özal would seem to have progressed far enough so that, regardless of his own political fortunes, private enterprise is sure to remain a major theme in the country's future. Previously, the decennial crises in Turkey's *étatist* economy had exposed the political weaknesses of its First and Second Republics. Now the moves toward privatization at home and free trade abroad are beginning to create pressures for adjustment and opening up safety valves that will soften such shocks in the future. The resulting milder economic fluctuations, in turn, are likely to let moderate right-wing parties, such as those of Özal or Demirel, alternate as "ins" and "outs" with parties of the moderate left, such as İnönü's Social Democrats.

The American Connection and Turkey's Rhythm of Change

Turkey's cultural, social, and political transformation has gained momentum in the last two centuries, and at each stage the American contribution to that process has become more relevant and prominent.

The original impetus for Ottoman Turkey's Westernization, as noted above, was the desire to match Europe's growing military prowess. For their temporary alliances or longer-term administrative reform, the Ottomans relied on various European sources of aid, and they did well enough to delay the final collapse of their empire by as much as a century and a half (1768–1918). In commerce and higher education, French influence was intense from the early nineteenth century, and in military training, Prussian officers soon took the lead. Yet all such assistance from Europe was clearly motivated by power politics, with all its risks of sudden reversal or imperial domination. By contrast, the educational efforts of American missionaries seemed selfless. The fact that Halide Edib graduated from Istanbul's Robert College at a time when college degrees still were a rarity even among American women symbolizes the depth of that educational connection.

As Turkey launched its national revolution in 1919, Wilson's doctrine of self-determination was received as enthusiastically among Turks as it was among Armenians, Arabs, and other former Ottoman subjects—Halide Edib helped found a "Society for Wilson's Principles" in 1919. There also was keen interest, both in the sultan's government and among Atatürk's nationalists, in the idea of an American "mandate" over former Ottoman territories.

Atatürk, who had been careful to sidetrack that mandate proposal, later was to remark with some condescension: "Poor Wilson, he did not understand that lines which are not defended by the bayonet, by force, by honor and dignity, cannot be defended by any other principle."[8] Considering the animosity of Greeks, Turks, Armenians, Kurds, and Arabs at the time—and the difficulties Britain later experienced as a mandatory power in Palestine—it was presumably fortunate all around that nothing came of the idea of an American mandate in the Middle East. Instead, the U.S. Senate rejected the League of Nations, Wilson retreated from public life, and Washington went into its twenty-year cycle of isolationism. In Turkey it was left to Atatürk's leadership and the remaining Ottoman bayonets to defend national honor and establish an independent republic.

In the educational efforts that followed, Atatürk took occasion to consult with the American pragmatist philosopher John Dewey; and amidst the proliferating state educational institutions, the private Robert College and its affiliated schools made their characteristic and growing contribution to the training of future scientists, engineers, and businessmen.

The timing of Turkey's transition to democracy, as we noted, was prompted by President İnönü's hope for support from Washington for Turkey's desperate but determined stand against overwhelming Soviet pressure. Yet this impetus was sustained because it was the logical outgrowth of Atatürk's nationalist principles and educational efforts.[9] Soon, moreover, the transition to democracy generated its own competitive momentum—powerfully reinforced by a wide range of U.S. aid programs: better seeds, year-round irrigation, and tractors to encourage cash-crop farming; expansion of the national educational system from grade schools to vocational training and universities; grants for students and aspiring public figures to study in the United States; roads, harbors, and airports to intensify the network of transport and communication for both civilian and military uses. In those early decades following the Truman Doctrine, the Marshall Plan, and Turkey's entry into NATO, English (spoken with an American accent) overtook French and German as the leading foreign language among educated Turks. Soon, the English-speaking colony in Ankara became large enough to warrant the publication (since 1961) by enterprising Turkish journalists of an *Ankara Daily News*.

The liberal revolution that Turgut Özal's government has sought to initiate in the 1980s may in some measure be characterized as an American answer to Turkish problems: privatization of state enterprises; economic mobility of capital and labor across frontiers; televised contests among political leaders; and bids for the second Bosporus Bridge thrown wide open to international competition. But Turkey was ready for just such an answer. Among Özal's chief rivals, Erdal İnönü, as we noted, is a U.S.-trained scientist who can look back on a successful academic career at Turkey's two English-speaking universities; and Süleyman Demirel started his career as a hydroelectric engineer, Eisenhower Fellow, and "father of dams."

America's educational and foreign aid efforts and intermittent pronouncements on national self-determination or anti-Soviet containment thus came to reinforce, at crucial moments, the historic initiatives that Turkey had taken for its own compelling reasons. And indeed, the long-run strength of the U.S.-Turkish connection lies in this close and dynamic interplay of indigenous and foreign impulses on the Turkish scene.

The domestic pattern of change in Turkey has typically included three elements: a political decision, perhaps taken reluctantly and under duress, sketching out new cultural goals; a program of education instituted to move toward them; and the beneficiaries of that education giving growing momentum to the process of change far beyond those original goals.

Just so, a midnineteenth-century sultan sent some young officers to Paris for training in French, mathematics, and the arts of artillery—and one of the young trainees returned to Istanbul, imbued with enthusiasm for European romantic poetry and ready to start the first Turkish-language private newspaper. A generation later, one of his disciples was to join a conspiracy that succeeded in forcing on the sultan's successor the adoption of the Ottoman Empire's first written parliamentary constitution.[10]

Just so, Mustafa Kemal, the later Atatürk, sought to rescue what remained of the Ottoman Empire after its defeat in World War I by proclaiming "Today the nations of the whole world recognize only one sovereignty: national sovereignty";[11] and set out to build a new structure of government and a popular, Western-style system of education. Soon Turkish citizens firmly embraced their newly defined national identity, while the dynamic of mass education began to revolutionize the towns and villages of the country.

Just so, Atatürk's successor İnönü decided in the late 1940s that the logic of Atatürk's political ideals and the need for closer ties to the West required a transition from one-party rule to competitive, democratic elections. And despite a number of reverses through economic crises, political deadlocks, and military coups, that commitment to democracy was repeatedly vindicated by Turkey's citizen-voters, most recently and emphatically in the election of 1983.

And so, in the wake of that election, Prime Minister Turgut Özal has sought to launch his liberal revolution of competition, free enterprise, and open economic bridges to Europe and Asia—a policy facilitated by the massive presence of Turkish factory workers in West Germany and the growing flow of Turkish businessmen to the Middle East.

In the late 1940s, Turkey's determination to stand up to the Soviet Union set an example which the United States endorsed with the containment policy of the Truman Doctrine. Four decades later, Turkey and the United States can benefit from each other's diversified political and economic relations in the Middle East, including the Arab countries, Iran, and Israel. Ankara's recent policy is in full accord with the aim of peaceful pluralism—of encouraging that self-balancing peaceful play of Middle Eastern forces which in our better moments we have helped to reinforce.

In the late twentieth century, Turkish and American interests in the Middle East converge and coincide more closely than ever. Turkey remains a crucial barrier to Soviet expansion. Historically and strategically, culturally and commercially, Turkey is the West's bridge to a more peaceful Middle East.

Notes

Chapter One

1. The quotations are from two publications of the U.S. Helsinki Watch Committee, *Violations of the Helsinki Accords: Turkey* (New York, November 1986), p. 1, and *Freedom and Fear: Human Rights in Turkey: A Helsinki Watch Report* (New York, March 1986), p. 1. For an earlier account see Amnesty International's *Turkey: Testimony on Torture* (London: Amnesty International Publications, 1985).

2. See the three-page centerfold advertisement of Chase Manhattan Bank in *The Economist*, September 13, 1986: "Only a global power could bring two continents like Europe and Asia together. It took the people at Chase to engineer the $550 million financial structure to do it."

3. For details, see Chapter 5.

Chapter Two

1. The statement by Abdullah Cevdet in the journal *İçtihad* is quoted in Bernard Lewis, *The Emergence of Modern Turkey*, 2d ed. (London: Oxford University Press, 1968), p. 236; cf. my essay "The Roses and the Thorns," in D. A. Rustow and Trevor Penrose, *The Mediterranean Challenge, V: Turkey and the Community*, Sussex European Papers no. 10 (Brighton: University of Sussex, 1981).

2. The law on the new alphabet, adopted by the Grand National Assembly on November 3, 1928, made it illegal to use Arabic letters in public print after December 1. An amusing illustration of the uncompromising time schedule is provided by the Assembly's own yearbook for 1928. From pages 1 to 278, it is printed in the Arabic script, with pages turning from left to right; then, shifting abruptly in midsentence, it is printed in the new Latin alphabet from pages 279 to 302, although the pages continue to turn from left to right. See *Türkiye Büyük Millet Meclisi Yıllığı: Devre 2, İçtima 1, 1928* (Ankara: TBMM Matbaası). Obviously, the Assembly and its printing press had to set a good example in obeying their own law.

3. The majority of these European professors were refugees from Nazi Germany—among them Paul Hindemith, who helped found the Music Teachers' College in Ankara.

Among the first professors at the new University of Istanbul in 1933 was my father, the economist and sociologist Alexander Rüstow, who felt "deeply indebted to the new Turkey, brought into. . .the orbit of Western culture by Atatürk, for the privilege of having been able to devote myself to scholarly pursuits" at a time when Germany's "stifling atmosphere after Hitler's conquest left me no air to breathe." See his book *Freedom and Domination: A Historical Critique of Civilization*, Engl. trans. ed. D. A. Rustow (Princeton: Princeton University Press, 1981), p. xxiii.

4. Eleanor Bisbee, *The New Turks* (Philadelphia: University of Pennsylvania Press, 1951), p. 87.

5. As part of a common Ottoman heritage, it is also the national drink in Greece, where it is known as *oozo*, and among Arabs, who call it *arak*.

6. A new obscenity law of March 1986, however, caused newsstand copies of *Playboy* to be discretely packaged in plastic covers emblazoned with the well-known bunny symbol.

7. "Women Managers and Turkey's Sexist Society," *Wall Street Journal*, May 15, 1985.

8. The only previous instance of a Turkish woman party leader was that of Behice Boran, who in 1970 became chairman of the communist Turkish Labor Party.

9. Among these patriotic holidays, the Youth and Sports Holiday commemorates Atatürk's landing in Anatolia (May 19, 1919) to head the incipient nationalist movement—the same day being later declared his birthday. The National Sovereignty Holiday is a one-and-a-half-day celebration recalling the convening of the Grand National Assembly in Ankara (April 23, 1920). Victory Day celebrates the decisive battle against the Greek forces in Turkey's War of Independence (August 30, 1922). And the proclamation of the Turkish Republic in 1923 is commemorated by a two-and-a-half-day holiday (October 28 to 30), with patriotic speeches and ceremonies reminiscent of America's Fourth of July. Note, however, that the Candy and Sacrifice Holidays are longer than any of these.

10. For an apparent agnostic such as Atatürk to presume to change the language of the public prayer call from Arabic to "pure Turkish" had always been particularly shocking to Muslim sensibilities; for it had substituted a contrived idiom for the very language in which God had revealed himself to Muhammad, and an obsolescent Turkish word for the authentic Arabic name of Allah.

11. The exception was the 1973 election; cf. Chapter 4.

12. See Klaus-Detlev Grothusen, ed., *Türkei: Südosteuropa–Handbuch IV* (Göttingen: Vandenhoeck & Ruprecht, 1985), p. 605, which adds that less plausible estimates range as high as 40 percent; for the 20 percent figure see, e.g., S. Vaner, "Etat, Société et Violence Politique en Turquie

(1975–1980)," in Equipe de Recherche sur la Turquie (E.R.T.), *Bulletin de Liaison*, no. 2 (Paris: Fondation Nationale des Sciences Politiques, Mai 1985), p. 4n. Precise data are lacking, because Sunni census officials have not taken official cognizance of the divisions or heterodoxies in Islam. By contrast, the census takers of 1935 and 1945 felt no compunction in establishing the presence in Turkey of a minute group (.003 percent of total residents) belonging to "no religion" (*dinsiz*).

13. Ursula Spuler-Stegemann in Grothusen, op. cit., pp. 606–07.

14. The full set of five basic religious obligations for the believing Muslim are professing the creed, saying five daily prayers while bowing to Mecca, fasting during Ramadan, giving to the poor, and (for those who can afford it) making the pilgrimage to Mecca.

15. Bisbee notes that since Islam (like Judaism) "forbids the picturing of any human or angelic forms. . .during the *Mevlud*, any such pictures or photographs are removed or draped. At the same time, however, camera fans may be snapping pictures of the ceremony and the people engaged in it." Op. cit., p. 138.

16. The patriarchs and grand rabbis who headed these *millets* stood in rank just below the Islamic *şeyhülislâm*. As the Ottoman Empire dissolved, the size of the *millets* was reduced through the secession of Christian Balkan nations and then of Arab countries (1804–1908, 1918); through occasional intense ethnic conflict (as between Turks and Armenians in 1896 and 1915); and through the large-scale population exchange with Greece under the peace treaty of 1923. At the time of the Republic's first census, the proportion of non-Muslims in the Turkish population was 2.6 percent; by 1960 it had declined, through voluntary emigration and because of higher Muslim birth rates, to only 1.0 percent.

17. Questions about mother tongue have been omitted from subsequent censuses. For a balanced discussion of the available information, see Ruşen Keleş, "Population Structure," in Grothusen, op. cit., p. 475f.

Chapter Three

1. There also is Iraqi oil, shipped by pipeline across Turkey to the Mediterranean. That amount has vastly increased since the outbreak of the Iraq-Iran war in 1980 and the completion of a second pipeline from Iraq through Turkey to the Mediterranean. Some of this oil is reexported as crude petroleum, and some processed in Turkish refineries for domestic consumption or reexport.

2. The military junta of 1960 was not unmindful of the corporate interest of army officers, and soon the Army Mutual Assistance Foundation (OYAK with its Turkish initials) became a major holding company. One of its subsidiaries, an assembly plant for Renault cars, represents the third-largest foreign investment in Turkey. This close association of military leaders or their families with major industrial enterprises continues

under President Evren in the 1980s.

3. As one thoughtful analyst of the Turkish economic scene has suggested, one of the "objectives of the bureaucratic and political leadership" has been "to attain. . .national autarky for historical and military as well as economic reasons." See Asim Erdilek, *Direct Foreign Investment in Turkish Manufacturing*, Kieler Studien 169 (Tübingen: Mohr, 1984), p. 228.

4. William M. Hale, "Turkish Industry and the EEC," *Orient*, vol. 26, no. 2 (June 1985), pp. 168–80 at 169.

5. The number of workdays lost to strikes rose dramatically from 671,000 in 1973 to 1.4 million in 1977—and as much as 4.3 million in 1980.

Chapter Four

1. See the vivid report by Marvine Howe, *The New York Times*, September 19, 1980, p. 2.

2. Under the 1982 constitution (provisional article 4) ex-premiers Demirel and Ecevit and other executive committee members of the pre-1980 parties are forbidden to participate in politics until 1993, and other members of the 1977–80 parliament until 1988. In addition, the leaders of the right-wing nondemocratic groups, Necmettin Erbakan of the National Salvation Party and Alpaslan Türkeş of the Nationalist Action Party, were tried under ordinary criminal law, but acquitted in 1985.

3. In campaigning for his True Path Party for the by-election that fall, Demirel stressed the role of the military in a strong state—but also was reported to have sent a private, veiled warning to President Evren that, as a private citizen after 1989, he "might have to face the consequences of his actions." See the report of David Barchard, *Financial Times*, October 1, 1986.

4. The others were General Cemal Gürsel (1961–66, previously head of the 1960 military junta), General Cevdet Sunay (1966–73), Admiral Fahri Korutürk (1973–80), and General Kenan Evren (head of the 1980 junta and president since November 1982). The sole civilian was Celâl Bayar (1950–60); see Chapter 3.

5. The above account is based in part on a private interview with İnönü in 1954, when I inquired in detail into the motivation of his decision announced in 1945 and his reaction to the 1950 election. He indicated that he assumed that his party would continue in office for perhaps a decade longer, and added with feeling, "I never expected to see so much ingratitude."

6. Specifically to the d'Hondt list system common in continental Europe rather than the Hare system of single transferable votes familiar from some American cities. Hare dissolves all party cohesion and encourages personal independence and political moderation. D'Hondt gives the parties complete control over candidate lists; hence it makes the individual candidate quite powerless—and instead encourages the breakup of large

parties into tightly organized smaller ones. In Turkey, there were minor adjustments within the d'Hondt system on technical points such as threshold and pooling of remainders; the changes of the 1970s tended to split the parties worse. The 1983 election, on the contrary, was held under a law that divided the provinces into smaller constituencies and left unrepresented those parties that had no national base or received less than 10 percent of the vote; and those same provisions favoring the larger parties were further reinforced by an amendment in 1986.

7. In one flagrant instance, in Demirel's coalition government of July 1977, a representative of the Nationalist Movement Party of Alpaslan Türkeş was put in charge of the ministry of customs and monopolies—even though that party was believed to have close ties with drug-smuggling activities from Turkey across Bulgaria and into Europe.

8. On the principle of *étatisme*, or government direction of a mixed public-private economy, see Chapter 3.

9. Many of these formed the Freedom Party of 1955 and the New Turkey Party of 1961, later ending up in the Republican People's or Reliance parties.

10. The 1983 elections, when fines were imposed for nonparticipation, are omitted from this calculation. For voting percentages and seats obtained by the parties, see Fig. I: "The Turkish Popular Vote, 1950–1986," on page 69.

Chapter Five

1. William Hale, "Turkey, NATO and the Middle East," in Richard Lawless, ed., *Foreign Policy Issues in the Middle East*, Occasional Papers no. 28 (University of Durham, Centre for Middle Eastern and Islamic Studies, 1985), p. 44.

2. On the contrary, the government at times takes advantage of the prevailing foreign policy consensus to exile high-placed critics to minor, faraway diplomatic posts. This, as we saw, is what the 1960 junta did with its authoritarian minority, including Colonel Türkeş.

3. From 1920 to 1983, the average tenure was twenty-eight months for foreign ministers, twenty-six months for premiers, and only seventeen months for other ministries established in 1920. My calculations from M. Orhan Bayrak, *(1920–1984) Türkiyeyi Kimler Yönetti?* (Istanbul: Milliyet, 1984). The averages for the post-1983 period are considerably higher. The records at the foreign office are held by Tevfik Rüştü Aras (1925–38) and Şükrü Saracoğlu (1938–42).

4. University professors were prominent among the foreign ministers of the parliamentary governments from 1950 to 1980, including Fuad Köprülü, a Middle Eastern historian of world renown (1950–57); and the political scientists Turan Güneş (1974) and Gündüz Okçün (1977, 1978–79). The precedent followed since 1980, of a foreign ministry headed by

career officials, was established by the military or quasi-military regimes of 1960–61 and 1971–73.

5. At one point during the War of Independence, Atatürk severely reprimanded a general who was about to pursue the defeated Greek army across Turkey's internationally recognized boundary into Western Thrace. The fact that 200 miles beyond that border lay Atatürk's own birthplace of Salonica lends poignancy to this self-limitation in victory.

6. Quincy Wright, *A Study of War*, 2d ed. (Chicago: University of Chicago Press, 1965), p. 653, calculates that the Ottoman Empire, from 1450 to 1900, was at war an average of 30.5 years out of every half century.

7. The threat became clear in retrospect when the U.S. Department of State published the papers prepared by Foreign Minister V. M. Molotov in the German-Soviet negotiations of November 1940, which contained the following passage: "The Soviet Union declares that its territorial aspirations center" on "the area south of Batum and Baku in the general direction of the Persian Gulf." See J. C. Hurewitz, *The Middle East and North Africa in World Politics*, vol. II (New Haven: Yale University Press, 1979), pp. 559–62.

8. Ankara broke off diplomatic relations with Nazi Germany in August 1944, and declared war on the Axis early in 1945, in time to be invited to San Francisco as a founding member of the United Nations.

9. See the recollections of Mussolini's foreign minister, Galeazzo Ciano, *Diplomatic Papers* (London: Oldham, 1948), p. 435.

10. The statements are quoted by D. A. Rustow, "The Foreign Policy of the Turkish Republic," in *Foreign Policy in World Politics*, R.C. Macridis, ed. (Englewood Cliffs, N.J.: Prentice-Hall, 1958), p. 307.

11. Since the days of the Baghdad Pact of 1958, however, these relations have been reduced to the subambassadorial, chargé d'affaires level. A further downgrading took place in response to Israel's annexation of East Jerusalem in 1980—and a converse upgrading in 1986.

12. George W. Ball, *The Past Has Another Pattern: Memoirs* (New York: Norton, 1982), p. 345.

13. The crucial paragraph read: "I hope you will understand that your NATO allies have not had a chance to consider whether they have an obligation to protect Turkey against the Soviet Union if Turkey takes a step which results in Soviet intervention, without the full consent and understanding of its NATO allies." Those allies, of course, included Greece. For the full text of the Johnson letter of June 5, 1964, see *Middle East Journal*, summer 1966, pp. 386–93.

14. The relevant passages of the Treaty of Guarantee of 1960 (agreed at Zurich in 1959) read: "Greece, the United Kingdom and Turkey. . .recognise and guarantee the independence. . .of Cyprus, and also the state of affairs established by the Basic Articles of its Constitution" (art. 2). "In the event of any breach of the provisions of the present Treaty. . .each of the three guaranteeing Powers reserves the right to take action with the

sole aim of re-establishing the state of affairs established by the present Treaty" (art. 3).

15. The latter move took Ankara by surprise, and was prompted by Denktash's desire both to outmaneuver domestic opponents among the Turkish-Cypriots and to make use of the interregnum between military and civilian governments in Ankara. Turkey itself and Pakistan became the only countries to extend recognition.

16. Henry Kissinger, *Years of Upheaval* (Boston: Little, Brown, 1982), p. 1190.

17. Ibid., p. 1192.

18. Quoted in Ellen B. Laipson, *Congressional-Executive Relations and the Turkish Arms Embargo*, Congress and Foreign Policy Series, no.3, Foreign Affairs Committee Print (June 1981), p. 33.

19. In an interview with Atatürk (Mustapha Kemal Pasha) printed on the front page of the *Los Angeles Examiner*, August 1, 1926, he is quoted as sharply condemning the circles responsible for a recent assassination attempt on him, referring to them as "those left-overs from the former Young Turkey Party, who should have been made to account for the lives of millions of our Christian subjects who were ruthlessly driven en masse from their houses and massacred." Perhaps it is also relevant to note that no Jewish or Israeli organization has ever suggested that Hitler's Holocaust might justify a campaign of assassinations against West German diplomats—although some Armenians in response point to Turkey's failure to acknowledge any guilt, as Germany did through its program of reparations for victims of Nazi persecution.

20. But note that Turkey routinely accepts the ICO resolutions only with explicit reservation of its own constitutional provisions on secularism and strict separation of religion and state.

Chapter Six

1. See Bernard Gwertzman's report to *The New York Times*, March 24, 1986.

2. Specifically, Israel's de facto boundaries since the evacuation of the Sinai peninsula (and except for the annexation of the Golan Heights) are those drawn for the Palestine mandate in 1920–22. Otherwise, the only significant boundary changes are the merger of Nejd and Hijaz in the Kingdom of Saudi Arabia (1926), and the transfer, noted earlier, of the Alexandrette-Hatay district from Syria to Turkey (1938–39).

3. On Turkey's relations with Israel, see George E. Gruen, "Turkey's Relations with Israel and Its Arab Neighbors," *Middle East Review*, vol. 17, no. 3 (spring 1985), pp. 33–43. Note also that, in the wake of the terrorist bombing of the Istanbul synagogue of December 1986, Turkish law enforcement authorities cooperated fully with their Israeli and American counterparts; see the report by Judith Miller, "The Istanbul Synagogue

Massacre: An Investigation" in *The New York Times Magazine*, January 4, 1987, p. 14ff.

4. See *The New York Times*, September 6, 1986.

5. See Chapter 4, note 3.

6. For an American assessment of Turkey's progress, see Jeri Laber and Alice M. Henkin, "In Turkey: A Gain for Rights," *The New York Times*, December 24, 1985.

7. Organization for Economic Cooperation and Development, *Economic Outlook* (December 1985), p. 20.

8. Quoted from Atatürk's 1926 memoirs by D. A. Rustow, "The Army and the Founding of the Turkish Republic," *World Politics*, vol. 11, no. 4 (July 1959), p. 536.

9. In his speech on first arriving at his future capital of Ankara, Atatürk emphasized that the nationalist movement must "begin [its] work from the village. . .the neighborhood and. . .the individual." Quoted in D. A. Rustow, "Atatürk as Founder of a State," in *Philosophers and Kings*, D. A. Rustow, ed. (New York: Braziller, 1970), p. 222.

10. On İbrahim Şinasi and Namık Kemal, see Bernard Lewis, *The Emergence of Modern Turkey*, 2d ed. (London: Oxford University Press, 1968), Chap. V.

11. In the speech cited in note 9, above.

Appendix

Turkey: A Statistical Profile

	1960	1970	1980	1985*
POPULATION (million, midyear)	27.8	35.6	44.7	51.4
Population Increase (% net annual)	2.9	2.5	2.1	2.0
Life Expectancy (years at birth)	55.0	55.0	61.8	64.0
Urban Population (% of total)	31.9	38.5	43.9	45.5
Literacy (% adults)	38.0	51.3	68.8	—
Newspaper Circulation (per 1,000 people)	51.3	40.6	89.1	—
TV Sets (per 1,000 people)	—	1.8	75.3	119.0
ECONOMY				
Agricultural Employment (% of total)	78.5	67.7	53.5	—
Gross Domestic Product (billion US$)	5.7	12.8	56.9	49.7
Per Capita GDP (US$)	207	363	1,281	1,160
GDP Growth Rate (% per year)	—	4.9	-1.0	3.9
Number of Motor Vehicles (thousands)	247	586	1,047	1,282
Consumer Prices (% annual change)	9.5	6.1	32.9	42.4
Currency Value (TL per US$)	9.0	14.9	70.0	518.3
FOREIGN TRADE AND PAYMENTS				
Exports (million US$)	321	588	3,621	8,255
Agricultural Exports (% of total)	81†	75	58	22
Imports (million US$)	468	850	7,606	11,230
Workers' Remittances (million US$)	—	273	2,071	1,850
Balance of Payments (million US$)	-139	-172	-2,983	-1,013
Total U.S. Aid (grants, loans; economic, military; million US$)	222	272	406	734
Total Foreign Debt (million US$)	—	1,896	15,729	15,886
Debt Service (payments of principal and interest, million US$)	65	171	1,019	3,560

* or latest year available   †1961

	1960	1970	1980	1985*

ARMED FORCES

Armed Forces (number of men,

	1960	1970	1980	1985*
thousands)	500	478	569	630
Military Expenditures (million US$)	266	579	2,442	3,214
Military Expenditures (% of GDP)	4.7	4.3	4.3	4.4

* or latest year available

Sources:

Grothusen, K.D., ed., *Türkei: Südosteuropa–Handbuch IV* (Göttingen: Vandenhoeck & Ruprecht, 1985)

International Monetary Fund, *International Financial Statistics* (monthly)

Legum, C., et al., *Middle East Contemporary Survey 1985–86* (New York: Holmes & Meier, 1987)

OECD Economic Surveys: Turkey (Paris: OECD, various dates)

Stockholm International Peace Research Institute, *World Armaments and Disarmament: SIPRI Yearbook* (London: Taylor & Francis, annual)

Türkiye İstatistik Yıllığı 1985—Statistical Yearbook of Turkey (Ankara: State Institute of Statistics, annual)

United Nations Statistical Yearbook (annual)

USAID, *US Overseas Loans and Grants* (various dates)

World Bank, *World Debt Tables* (annual)

_____, *World Development Report*, 3rd ed. (New York: Oxford University Press, 1986)

_____, *World Tables*, 3rd ed. (Washington, D.C., 1984)

For Further Reading

Chapter One. Bridge over the Bosporus

Ferenc A. Vali, *Bridge Across the Bosporus: The Foreign Policy of Turkey* (Baltimore: Johns Hopkins University Press, 1971), includes a lively account of the opening of the Bosporus Bridge as a new link to Europe. For a more recent general presentation, see George S. Harris, *Turkey: Coping With Crisis* (Boulder: Westview, 1985), which emphasizes historical background and recent political trends. A unique compendium of information on Turkish society, economy, and domestic and foreign policy can be found in the volume edited by Klaus-Detlev Grothusen, *Türkei: Südosteuropa–Handbuch IV—Turkey: Handbook on Southeastern Europe IV* (Göttingen: Vandenhoeck & Ruprecht, 1985), with individual chapters (in German or English) by leading Turkish, European, and American experts. This work includes detailed statistical tables, biographies of leading politicians, and an extensive bibliography. For updates, especially on domestic politics, see the annual publication edited by Colin Legum et al., *Middle East Contemporary Survey 1985–86* (New York: Holmes & Meier, 1987). The current edition, volume 10, contains a chapter on Turkey by W.F. Weiker.

Chapter Two. ". . .We Go to the West"

Bernard Lewis's balanced and well-written history, *The Emergence of Modern Turkey*, second edition (London: Oxford University Press, 1968), includes a sensitive account of the struggle for Westernizing reform in the declining Ottoman Empire. For a more detailed history, see Stanford J. Shaw and Ezel Kural Shaw, *Reform, Revolution, and Republic: The Rise of Modern Turkey*, vol. 2 in *History of the Ottoman Empire and Modern Turkey*, ed. S.J. Shaw (New York and London: Cambridge University Press, 1977).

In *Political Modernization in Japan and Turkey* (Princeton: Princeton University Press, 1964), Robert E. Ward and Dankwart A. Rustow, together with an international team of historians and social scientists, assess the varied responses of those two countries to the secular impact of Western civilization—a theme which has, in recent years, come under renewed public attention in Turkey. A lively account of the transition from Ottoman traditionalism to Westernization is provided in two volumes by the first Turkish woman college graduate and dissident contemporary of Atatürk; see Halide Edib, *Memoirs* (New York: Century, 1926) and *The Turkish Ordeal: Being the Further Memoirs of Halide Edib* (New York: Century, 1928). For a prominent American intellectual's account of Atatürk's revolution in the making, see John Dewey, *Impressions of Soviet Russia and the Revolutionary World: Mexico, China, and Turkey* (New York: New Republic, 1932). Eleanor Bisbee draws a sensitive and detailed picture of the impact of that reform program a generation later in *The New Turks: Pioneers of the Republic, 1920–1950* (Philadelphia: University of Pennsylvania Press, 1951).

The "Eastern Question" was the phrase in which British policymakers in the nineteenth century summed up their difficulty in spreading imperial control, with a minimum of military effort, through the region between the Mediterranean and India. A classic study by Arnold J. Toynbee, *The Western Question in Greece and Turkey*, second edition (Boston: Houghton Mifflin, 1923), deftly turns that perspective around to give a suggestive and well-documented analysis of the international scene on which Mustafa Kemal (the later Atatürk) entered to transform the remnants of the defeated Ottoman Empire into a Turkish national state.

The best biography of Kemal Atatürk remains [John Patrick Douglas Balfour] Lord Kinross, *Atatürk: A Biography of Mustafa Kemal, Father of Modern Turkey* (New York: Morrow, 1965). Vamik D. Volkan and Norman D. Itzkowitz's "psycho-biography," *The Immortal Atatürk* (Chicago: University of Chicago Press, 1984), offers fascinating glimpses of intimate personal life—at times at the expense of relevant political or historical perspective. Ali Kazancigil and Ergun Özbudun, *Atatürk: Founder of a State* (London: C. Hurst, 1981), and their scholarly coauthors offer a more balanced evaluation of Atatürk as victor in this century's first successful war of "national liberation" and founder of the Turkish Republic than do most other symposia honoring the centennial of his birth; see also D. A. Rustow, "Atatürk as Founder of a State" in *Philosophers and Kings: Studies in Leadership*, ed. D. A. Rustow (New York: Braziller, 1970). My translation of the Turkish national anthem (quoted in Chapter 2), with commentary, will be found in my article "Mehmed Âkif's Independence Hymn: Religion and Nationalism in Atatürk's Movement of Liberation," *Journal of the American Institute for the Study of Middle East Civilizations* 1 (Autumn-Winter 1980–81): 112–17.

Walter F. Weiker, *The Modernization of Turkey: From Atatürk to the Present Day* (New York: Holmes & Meier, 1981), supports a detailed assessment of recent social and economic change with carefully selected statistics. Frederick W. Frey, *The Turkish Political Elite* (Cambridge: MIT Press, 1965), gives a very readable account of the changing social composition of Turkey's legislature in the one-party and democratic periods; while Leslie L.

Roos and Noralou Roos record the corresponding trends in Turkey's economic and social leadership in *Managers of Modernization: Organization and Elites in Turkey, 1950–1969* (Cambridge: Harvard University Press, 1971). Nicholas S. Ludington provides a succinct and well-informed discussion of the religious question in *Turkish Islam and the Secular State*, The Muslim World Today, Occasional Paper no. 1 (Washington: The American University—American Institute for Islamic Affairs, 1984).

Chapter Three. Turkey's Economy

The massive process of rural change in Turkey since the 1950s is presented in an economic study by Eva Hirsch, *Poverty and Plenty on the Turkish Farm* (New York: Columbia University Press, 1970); and in a lively case study by British anthropologist Paul Stirling, *Turkish Village* (London: Weidenfeld & Nicolson, 1965). See also Stirling's later account, "Cause, Knowledge, and Change: Turkish Village Revisited," in *Aspects of Modern Turkey*, ed. William M. Hale (London: Bowker, 1976), pp. 75–89. Stirling also produced a script, based on his second visit, for a 1983 BBC televison program. Joseph S. Szyliowicz, *Political Change in Rural Turkey: Erdemli* (The Hague: Mouton, 1966), traces the impact of competitive party politics on one small southern town; whereas Kemal H. Karpat, *The Gecekondu: Rural Migration and Urbanization* (London: Cambridge University Press, 1976), accompanies the villagers on their migration to the shantytowns of Turkey's major cities.

Nermin Abadan-Unat has edited two collective works, one on the even greater exodus of Turkish workers to Western Europe, *Turkish Workers in Europe, 1960–1975* (Leiden: Brill, 1976), and one on the changing place of women in Turkey itself, *Women in Turkish Society* (Leiden: Brill, 1981). German prejudices against Turkish immigrant workers are vividly portrayed by a German investigative reporter who for several months disguised himself to experience the life of the "down-and-out": Günter Wallraff, *Ganz Unten* (Cologne: Kiepenheuer & Witsch, 1985).

An early—optimistic and influential—assessment of Turkish economic prospects at the beginning of the massive U.S. economic aid program in the 1950s was given by Max Weston Thornburg and his coauthors in *Turkey: An Economic Appraisal* (New York: Twentieth Century Fund, 1949). Subsequent analyses of economic progress will be found in books by an American and an Israeli economist: Edwin J. Cohn, *Turkish Economic, Social, and Political Change* (New York: Praeger, 1970), and Zvi Yehuda Hershlag, *Turkey: The Challenge of Growth*, second edition (Leiden: Brill, 1968). The traditional obstacles to foreign trade and investment and their recent lifting are analyzed in two competent economic studies: Anne O. Krueger, *Foreign Trade Regimes and Economic Development: Turkey* (New York: National Bureau of Economic Research, 1974), and Asim Erdilek, *Direct Foreign Investment in Turkish Manufacturing* (Kieler Studien; Tübingen: Mohr, 1984).

The best single source for current statistical information is the annual report on Turkey in the Organization for Economic Cooperation and Development's Economic Surveys. The most recent issue of this series is *OECD Economic Surveys 1985/1986: Turkey* (Paris: OECD, May 1986). See also the statistical summaries by TÜSIAD (Turkish Industrialists' and Businessmen's Association), *The Turkish Economy* (Istanbul, annual), and by one of Turkey's leading banks, İs Bankasi, *Review of Economic Conditions* (Ankara, quarterly). The OECD's *Foreign Investment in Turkey* (Paris: OECD, 1983) provides a guide to relevant recent legislation.

Chapter Four. The Hard Road to Democracy

The best introductions to the domestic political scene are William M. Hale, *The Political and Economic Development of Modern Turkey* (New York: St. Martin's, 1981), and Frank Tachau, *Turkey: The Politics of Authority, Democracy, and Development* (New York: Praeger, 1984).

Among earlier analyses, Walter F. Weiker, *Political Tutelage and Democracy in Turkey: The Free Party and Its Aftermath* (Leiden: Brill, 1975), recounts Atatürk's half-hearted experiment with democracy in 1930; and Kemal H. Karpat, *Turkey's Politics: The Transition to a Multiparty System* (Princeton: Princeton University Press, 1959), concentrates on the political struggles of the late 1940s that led to the first free elections and change of party regime. D.A. Rustow assesses the opening years of Turkey's Second Republic in "Turkey's Second Try at Democracy," *Yale Review* 52 (Summer 1963): 518–38, and its approaching final crisis in "Turkey's Travails," *Foreign Affairs* 58 (Fall 1979): 82–102.

Feroz Ahmad, *The Turkish Experiment in Democracy, 1950–1975* (Boulder: Westview, 1977), gives a well-balanced analysis of the ups-and-downs of progress and setbacks; whereas Ergun Özbudun, *Social Change and Political Participation in Turkey* (Princeton: Princeton University Press, 1976), and Robert R. Bianchi, *Interest Groups and Political Development in Turkey* (Princeton: Princeton University Press, 1984), provide some of the essential social background. For an account of parties and elections in the pre-1980 period see the chapters on Turkey in Jacob M. Landau, Ergun Özbudun, and Frank Tachau, eds., *Electoral Politics in the Middle East: Issues, Voters and Elites* (London: Croom Helm/Stanford: Hoover Institution Press, 1980). On the specific effects of proportional representation in encouraging radicalism and stalemating the major parties, see William M. Hale, "The Role of the Electoral System in Turkish Politics," *International Journal of Middle Eastern Studies* 11, no. 3 (1980): 401–17

The difficulties of transition to democracy are discussed theoretically and comparatively, with specific references to Turkey, in D.A. Rustow, "Transitions to Democracy: Toward A Dynamic Model," *Comparative Politics* 2 (April 1970): 337–63; and Samuel P. Huntington, "Will More Countries Become Democratic?" *Political Science Quarterly* 99 (Summer 1984): 193–218. A detailed comparison of Turkey and Israel is given in D.A.

Rustow, "Elections and Legitimacy in the Middle East," *Annals of the American Academy of Political and Social Science* 482 (November 1985): 122–46. For a thoughtful discussion of the Ottoman and Kemalist legacies and their place in today's ideological discussion, see Metin Heper, *The State Tradition in Turkey* (North Humberside: Eothen Press, 1985).

George S. Harris has provided a scholarly study of Turkish communism in *The Origins of Communism in Turkey* (Stanford: Hoover Institution, 1967) and, more recently, in his article "The Left in Turkey," *Problems of Communism* 29 (July-August 1980). Jacob M. Landau examines the extreme right in *Pan-Turkism in Turkey: A Study of Irredentism* (London: Hurst, 1981). Binnaz Toprak, *Islam and Political Development in Turkey* (Leiden: Brill, 1981), gives a comprehensive and well-balanced account of the religious-conservative parties.

For good accounts of the crisis of the late 1970s and its resolution in 1980–83, see Udo Steinbach, *Kranker Wächter am Bosporus: Die Türkei als Riegel zwischen Ost und West* (Würzburg: Ploetz, 1979); Clement Henry Dodd, *The Crisis of Turkish Democracy* (North Humberside: Eothen Press, 1983); and Lucille W. Pevsner, *Turkey's Political Crisis: Background, Perspectives, Prospects*, (New York: Praeger, 1984).

There are a number of specialized studies on the political role of the Turkish military, including D.A. Rustow, "The Army and the Founding of the Turkish Republic," *World Politics* 11 (July 1959): 513–52; Walter F. Weiker, *The Turkish Revolution, 1960–1961: Aspects of Military Politics* (Washington: The Brookings Institution, 1963); and Metin Tamkoç, *The Warrior Diplomats: Guardians of National Security and the Modernization of Turkey* (Salt Lake City: University of Utah Press, 1976). For a thoughtful defense of that military-political role, see Nicholas S. Ludington and James W. Spain, "Dateline Turkey: The Case for Patience," *Foreign Policy* (Spring 1983): 150–68.

On the Evren junta's "shock" at the outcome of the 1983 general election, see the well-informed account of Kenneth Mackenzie, *Turkey in Transition: The West's Neglected Ally* (London: Institute for European Defence and Strategic Studies, 1984), especially pp. 9–13. For a broader impression of Turkey in the wake of that election, see Joseph Kraft, "Letter from Turkey," *The New Yorker*, October 15, 1984.

Chapters Five and Six. The Turkish-American Alliance; Turkey, the Middle East, and the West

The origins of the Truman Doctrine and the American-Turkish alliance are analyzed in a detailed, competent, and well-written history by Bruce R. Kuniholm, *The Origins of the Cold War in the Near East: Great Power Conflict and Diplomacy in Iran, Turkey, and Greece* (Princeton: Princeton University Press, 1980); whereas Joseph M. Jones, *The Fifteen Weeks* [February 5–June 21, 1947] (New York: Viking, 1955), provides a highly dramatic Washington perspective. On the earlier problems of Ankara's diplomacy in World War II, see Edward Weisband, *Turkish Foreign Policy 1943–1945: Small State Diplomacy and Great Power Politics* (Princeton: Princeton University Press, 1973), and Frank G. Weber, *The Evasive Neutral: Germany, Britain, and the Quest for a Turkish Alliance* (Columbia: University of Missouri Press, 1979). A thoughtful contemporary assessment of U.S. policy in the Middle East in the 1950s will be found in John C. Campbell, *Defense of the Middle East: Problems of American Foreign Policy*, revised edition (New York: Harper & Row/Council on Foreign Relations, 1960). On the earlier history of U.S.-Turkish relations, see Harry N. Howard, *Turkey: The Straits, and U.S. Policy* (Baltimore: Johns Hopkins University Press, 1974).

For competent analyses of tensions in U.S.-Turkish relations introduced by the missile crisis of 1962 and the Cyprus conflict, see George S. Harris, *Troubled Alliance: Turkish-American Problems in Historical Perspective, 1945–1971* (Washington: American Enterprise Institute, 1972); and Andrew Mango, *Turkey: A Delicately Poised Ally* (Beverly Hills: Sage, 1975). On the Jupiter missile crisis, see also Graham B. Allison, *Essence of Decision: Explaining the Cuban Missile Crisis* (Boston: Little, Brown, 1972). A comprehensive and incisive account of the origins of the Congressional embargo on aid to Turkey is given by Ellen B. Laipson, *Congressional Executive Relations and the Turkish Arms Embargo* (Foreign Affairs Committee Print; Washington: GPO, 1981), which also reviews the Congressional comments quoted in Chapter 5. James W. Spain, *American Diplomacy in Turkey* (New York: Praeger, 1984), recalls the tribulations and rewards of an ambassador during the restoration of cordial relations in the early 1980s.

A lively and balanced overview of the Cyprus conflict emerges from Christopher Hitchens, *Cyprus* (New York: Quartet Books, 1984). Some of its earlier phases are detailed in Stephen Xydis, *Cyprus: Reluctant Republic* (The Hague: Mouton, 1973), and Polyvios G. Polyviou, *Cyprus: Conflict and Negotiation, 1960–1980* (New York: Holmes & Meier, 1980). Necati M. Ertekün documents the official Turkish position in *The Cyprus Dispute and the Birth of the Turkish Republic of Northern Cyprus*, second edition (London: K. Rustem, 1984). The Aegean conflict is summarized in Andrew Wilson, *The Aegean Dispute* (Adelphi Papers; London: International Institute of Strategic Studies, 1980). The resulting regional and U.S. policy problems are searchingly analyzed in Theodore A. Coulombis, *The U.S. and Greece and Turkey: The Troubled Triangle* (New York: Praeger, 1983). See also Andre Borowiec, *The Mediterranean Feud* (New York: Praeger, 1983); Jonathan Alford, ed., *Greece and Turkey: Adversity in Alliance* (New York: St. Martin's/International Institute of Strategic Studies, 1984); and the memoirs of George W. Ball (who played a key role in the Cyprus crisis of 1963), *The Past Has Another Pattern* (New York: Norton, 1982). On the Armenians, see Christopher Walker, *Armenia: The Survival of a Nation* (London: Croom Helm, 1980), and Paul Wilkinson's article "Armenian Terrorism" in *The World Today*, September 1983, pp. 344–350.

On Turkish relations with the EEC see Deutsches Orient-Institut, *Tur-*

key and the European Community (Hamburg, 1985). On some of the earlier background, see D.A. Rustow, "Turkey and Europe: The Roses and the Thorns," in *Turkey and the Community*, Sussex European Papers no. 10 (Brighton: University of Sussex, 1981).

The strategic problems of the 1980s are sketched in recent monographs by Duygu B. Sezer, *Turkey's Security Policies*, Adelphi Papers no. 164 (London: International Institute of Strategic Studies, 1981) and Alvin Z. Rubinstein, *Soviet Policy Toward Turkey, Iran, and Afghanistan* (New York: Praeger, 1982).

Turkey's potential strategic role in the Middle East is discussed by Marcy Agmon, *Defending the Upper Gulf: Turkey's Forgotten Partnership*, EAI Papers (Marina del Rey, California: European American Institute, 1984); from a well-informed Turkish perspective, by Ali L. Karaosmanoglu, "Turkey's Security and the Middle East," *Foreign Affairs* 62 (Fall 1983): 157–75; and by a group of leading American and Turkish specialists in George S. Harris, ed., *The Middle East in Turkish-American Relations* (Washington: The Heritage Foundation, 1985). For the broader regional context, see the special issue on "Turkey and the Middle East" of *The Middle East Review* 17 (Spring 1985). For an elaboration of my views on U.S. Middle East policy, see my book *Oil and Turmoil: America Faces OPEC and the Middle East* (New York: Norton, 1982), especially p. 237ff., which stresses the need for "peaceful pluralism." Also see my articles, "Realignments in the Middle East," *Foreign Affairs* 63, no. 3, pp. 581–601, and "Safety in Numbers: Reflections on the Middle Eastern Balance of Power," in *Historian of the Middle East: Essays in Honor of Bernard Lewis* (Princeton: Darwin Press, 1987).

Index

About the Author

DANKWART A. RUSTOW is Distinguished Professor of Political Science and Sociology at the Graduate School of the City University of New York, and editor-in-chief of the quarterly journal *Comparative Politics*.

He received his early education in Germany and Turkey, graduated from Queens College and obtained his Ph.D. from Yale. Before joining the CUNY faculty, he taught at Princeton and Columbia universities and served on the senior staff at the Brookings Institution. He has been a visiting professor at Harvard, Yale, Heidelberg, The London School of Economics, The American University of Beirut, and other universities here and abroad.

Professor Rustow was elected vice president of the Middle East Studies Association of North America and of the American Political Science Association, and has been a consultant to the U.S. Department of State and other government agencies. In 1983 and 1985, he was co-chairman of the American-Soviet Symposium on the Contemporary Middle East, co-sponsored by the American Council of Learned Societies and the Soviet Academy of Sciences

Professor Rustow is the author of numerous books in the field of comparative and international politics, including *The Politics of Compromise* (1955); *A World of Nations* (1967); *Philosophers and Kings* (ed. 1970); *Middle Eastern Political Systems* (1971); *OPEC: Success and Prospects* (with J.F. Mugno, 1976); and *Oil and Turmoil: America Faces OPEC and the Middle East* (1982). His articles on contemporary history and political analyses have appeared in many scholarly and general publications, including *Foreign Affairs, Foreign Policy, Yale Review, The American Scholar, World Politics, The Encyclopedia of Islam, The New Leader, The New York Times, The Wall Street Journal*, and *The Times Literary Supplement*. They have been translated into Danish, French, German, Italian, Japanese, Spanish, Thai and Turkish.

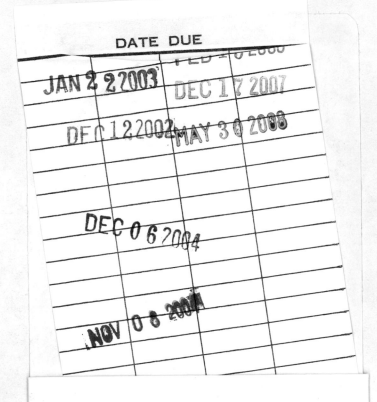